1 HOUR
INVEST$R

A BEGINNER'S GUIDE TO INVESTING WISELY IN STOCKS, MUTUAL FUNDS, AND BONDS

VISHAL REDDY

TCK PUBLISHING.COM

ISBN: 978-1-63161-068-4

Published by TCK Publishing
www.TCKpublishing.com

Get discounts and special deals on our best-selling books at
www.TCKpublishing.com/bookdeals

Sign up for Vishal Reddy's newsletter at
www.vishalreddyauthor.com/free

TABLE OF CONTENTS

DISCLAIMER

Investing in the stock market is an inherently risky venture, no matter the types of investments you make. At the time of writing, I do not own any of the financial securities mentioned in this book and thus neither recommend—nor advise against—any specific securities mentioned within this book. This book is a basic educational guide to investing, and any investing decisions on your part should be made in consultation with a professional financial advisor. I make no claims of any securities mentioned herein, in terms of future profits, losses, or general performance. Investing can lead to financial losses, up to and including your entire invested capital. My words shall be construed solely as entertainment and not as a recommendation to buy or sell any particular financial security or to invest in any particular sector, industry, or asset class. Invest at your own risk.

INTRODUCTION

Does the stock market seem like a foreign world to you? When you see financial experts on television, does their nonstop jargon just fly over your head? Don't you wish you understood how the stock market works so you could make money too?

With this book, your wish has been granted!

In *One Hour Investor*, you will learn to master the basic fundamentals of investing. Whether you want to learn about stocks, bonds, mutual funds, 401(k)s, or investing for long-term financial freedom, this is the book for you. Written in a very accessible style for beginners, *One Hour Investor* is your handy guide to investing in the stock market and beginning your financial journey.

Whether you're a teen or twenty-something who wants to know how to save for your eventual retirement, a senior who wants a steady stream of income, or anybody in between, the answers are within this book.

One Hour Investor is the quick and easy beginner's guide to investing. It covers all sorts of financial instruments as well as basic financial concepts you'll need to know to invest wisely. You don't need to be a math whiz or have an MBA to understand anything in this book. It's all laid out for you in plain English with examples so you can learn what you need to know about investing. There's even a handy glossary at the end of the book if you ever need to look up a financial term or concept.

You can stop worrying about your financial future. By picking up this book, you'll have taken the first steps of your journey to financial success. So, what are you waiting for? In just one hour, you could possess enough financial knowledge for a lifetime of successful investing!

CHAPTER 1

WHAT EVERYONE SHOULD KNOW ABOUT INVESTING

Here's a pop quiz for you: What's the one thing that we *all* possess, regardless of our station in life? Here's a hint: it's actually *more valuable* than money. The answer is *time*.

Now you might be thinking, "How can time be more valuable than money?" Well, there are two reasons. First, time is something we can never get back, unlike money. You can always earn more money, but you can never earn back time once it's gone. Second, time is what allows your money to grow for you so you can create wealth and financial freedom. This phenomenon is called the **time value of money (TVM)**, and it's the most important principle you must understand to become a successful investor.

Time Value of Money (TVM)

The time value of money means that a dollar today is worth more than a dollar in the future. How does this work? Let's start with a basic example. Pretend you have two choices. Either I give you $100 right now or I give you $100 next year. Which do you choose?

Obviously, everybody prefers money sooner than later. But the key difference here is that the $100 I'm giving you right now isn't going to be spent right away. That's because you are going to *invest* it. And that's where TVM comes in.

If you take my $100 right now, you could put it in your bank account and have it earn, let's say, 2% interest per year. So after one year, your $100 becomes $102. That means you made a 2% profit because $2 divided by $100 equals 2% (Figure 1).

But what if you accepted my $100 a year from now and invested it in the same bank account? You'd still make a 2% profit, but it happened a year later. In other words, you missed out on your money growing sooner rather than later, so you end up with less money (Figure 2). TVM means that the sooner you invest money, the bigger it will grow.

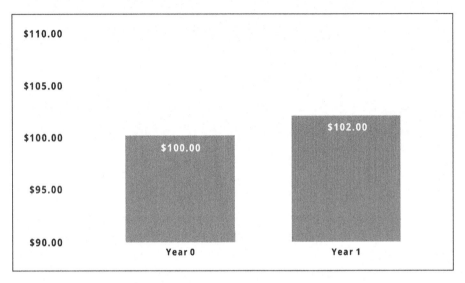

Figure 1

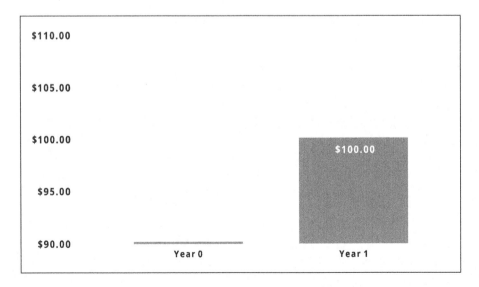

Figure 2

Now let's go further. If you had taken my $100 immediately and put it in your 2% interest-earning bank account, you'd have $102 after one year, right? So, what would happen if you kept the $102 in your bank account for another year? Well, it would grow by even more than $2 because of compound interest.

Compound Interest

Compound interest is the interest earned on your principal and previously earned interest. In Year 1, you only earned simple interest because the interest only applied to your principal of $100. In Year 2, the 2% interest is applied to your principal and interest of $102 ($100 principal plus $2 interest).

A quick calculation shows that $102 × 1.02% = $104.04. Do you see the magic of compound interest now? The $104.04 balance means you've made a 4.04% profit in two years just by doing nothing. Because compound interest applies to your principal and earned interest, you are making more money just by letting your money stay in your account. Your interest from Year 1 produced an extra 4-cent profit for you. Now that's not much money, but over time compound interest grows incredibly fast, especially at higher interest rates and over longer periods of time.

Now imagine you want to keep investing, so you leave the $104.04 in that same account and let it accrue (grow) at 2% interest every year for 10 years. Using a financial calculator, enter $100 for the present value (or PV) or Starting Principal, 2 for the interest (or INT), 10 for the number of periods (or N), and 0 for payment (or PMT). Now select future value (or FV) or Calculate. The result reveals that after 10 years, the initial $100 you invested is now worth $121.90. So in 10 years, you've made $21.90 by doing absolutely nothing—a return on investment (ROI) of 21.90%. This is because $21.90/$100 = 21.90%.

Note: You can find a financial calculator online for free—this is a good one: **www.calculator.net/finance-calculator.html**

Now let's assume you kept the $100 in the same account for 20 years. Enter the same numbers as before (100 for PV, 2 for INT), but enter the number 20 for N. Now select FV. That means that after 20 years at 2% interest, your $100 is now worth $148.59—a 48.59% ROI.

Let's go further and assume you leave the $100 in there for 30 years. Your $100 turns into $181.14—an 81.14% ROI.

And finally, let's say you leave the $100 in the account for 40 years. What happens then? Your $100 becomes $220.80—an ROI of 120.80% (Figure 3).

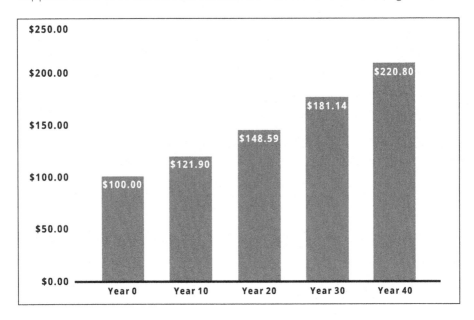

Figure 3

Did you notice the pattern in the previous examples? The longer you kept the money in your account as it earned interest, the more money you ended up with. That's the time value of money. **Essentially, time is more valuable than money for an investor because time is the most important factor in making money grow.**

But wait. Did you notice something else in those examples? Look at the series of ROIs again. What do you see? Not only did your ROI grow as time went on, but after Year 40, your ROI was over 100%. This brings us to another key concept: Given enough time, compound interest means the majority of your investment gains will come from interest, not principal. Don't believe me? Find a financial calculator online and enter $100 for your principal, 2% for your interest rate, and 50 years for your number of periods. Then do the same thing but with 60 years for your number of periods. The amount of interest you've earned over those years accounts for an increasing share of your overall balance. That's the power of time and compound interest. But TVM and compound interest don't just apply to leaving your money in the bank. They also apply when you're investing in stocks, mutual funds, and similar instruments, which we will discuss shortly. And since these other investments can earn you more than 2% on average, your money can grow a whole lot faster than it did in the examples we just covered.

Before we move on to other concepts, I want to show you a fun (though implausible) exercise just to show you how important time is in growing your money. You may be familiar with the animated TV series *Futurama*, in which a young pizza delivery boy named Fry is accidentally transported 1,000 years into the future. In one of the early episodes of the show, Fry mentions that he had less than a dollar in his bank account 1,000 years ago. So, he heads to the bank and is shocked to find that compound interest that's accrued over 1,000 years has made him rich beyond his wildest dreams.

So here's the exercise based on *Futurama*. On the financial calculator website, enter $100 for your principal, 2% for the annual interest, and 0 for PMT, just like before. Now enter 1,000 years for the number of periods (N) and select future value (or FV) or Calculate. In 1,000 years, your $100 earning 2% a year would be worth $39,826,465,165.84! If only time machines were real, anyone could become a billionaire!

Rule of 72

Now back to reality. What if you just want to find out how long it would take for your money to double? In other words, how long would it take to make a 100% profit? There's a simple calculation for that called the Rule of 72. **The Rule of 72 states that the number of years (or periods) required to double an investment's value is calculated by dividing 72 by the investment's annual return on investment (ROI).**

Here's an example. You put $1,000 in a particular investment that has an average ROI of 6% per year. So divide 72 by 6 and what do you get? 12. That means if you invested $1,000 in something that has an average ROI of 6% per year, it would take 12 years to double your money to $2,000. A very simple rule of thumb to remember is this: The higher your ROI, the less time it will take to double your money. For example, if that same investment had a 10% ROI, then dividing 72 by 10 results in 7.2—you would double your $1,000 in just 7.2 years. Simple, isn't it?

Present Value versus Future Value

Now let's look at the concepts of present value (PV) and future value (FV). Imagine that you want to save up $10,000 for a globe-trotting vacation five years from now. You do have some money saved up, and you would like to invest it in something with a 4% annual ROI so that it's worth $10,000 in five years. How much money would you need to invest today so that you have the $10,000 you need for your trip in five years?

To find the answer, enter the following information into a financial calculator: 5 for the number of years (or N), $10,000 for the future value (or FV), 0 for your PMT, and 4 for the ROI (or INT). Then select PV (present value) or Calculate, and the result is $8,219.26.

Note: Some financial calculators may return a value that is one cent off because of rounding.

So what does this mean? Basically, if your future value is $10,000 (the amount you need in the future), you need it in five years, and you want to invest in something with a 4% annual ROI, then you would need to invest $8,219.26 today. **This number is your present value, which is the current value of a future sum of money**. So, if you have a specific financial goal (future value) and you know your timeframe (number of periods) and you know the ROI (interest) of your investment, it's very easy to find out how much you need to invest today—your present value.

This process of finding your present value is known as discounting. That's because you are discounting a known future value to the present to find the smaller present value that you need today.

The formula also works in the opposite direction. Say you had $8,219.26 in your bank account right now. You want to invest it in something with a 4% annual ROI, and you want to know how much it will be worth in five years. On the financial calculator, enter $8,219.26 for your present value, 5 for your number of periods, 0 for your PMT, and 4 for your ROI (or INT). Now select FV (future value). What do you get? $10,000. **This process of finding a future value is known as compounding**. That's because you are taking a known present value and compounding it with a specific ROI and time period to find that larger future value. Compounding is the opposite of discounting.

In fact, as long as you know any three of these four values—N, INT, FV or PV— you can find the missing fourth value with your financial calculator. Remember, N is the number of years or periods you'll be investing, INT is the interest rate or rate of return you'll be investing at, FV is the future value of your money at the end of the investing period, and PV is the present value of the money you'll be investing today.

Try it out for yourself. Enter $8,219.26 for your present value, $10,000 for your future value, 0 for your PMT, and 4 for your ROI. Now calculate N (number of periods) and what do you get? Five years! With a financial calculator, it's very easy to find out the relevant information for your financial plans.

Consistent Payments (PMT)

Let's take this knowledge one step further. On any financial calculator, there is a fifth value that is sometimes entered or is derived from the other four values. This is the payment value, often abbreviated PMT, as I mentioned before. This value generally refers to ongoing deposits you make in a stock, mutual fund, or exchange-traded fund (ETF).

Let's pretend that you invest $1,000 right now in one of those three investment vehicles and you assume it will have an annual ROI of 3%. You will keep your $1,000 invested for 20 years. So you would just enter $1,000 for the present value, 3 for the ROI, and 20 for the number of periods, which gives you a future value of $1,806.11. So if you invest $1,000 and have a 3% annual ROI, you would have $1,806.11 in 20 years, right? But remember: that future value of $1,806.11 assumes you are not investing any additional money at all beyond that first $1,000.

But what if you do want to deposit more money into this investment to make the future value even bigger? In fact, what if you want to deposit a specific amount of money at regular intervals? Well, that is where the PMT value comes in.

Take the original information we had: a $1,000 present value, a 3% annual ROI, and a time period of 20 years. Now let's say you want to invest an additional $200 every year for 20 years into this stock, mutual fund, or ETF. On your financial calculator, enter $1,000 for the present value, 3 for the ROI, 20 for the number of periods, and finally 200 for PMT. Now select future value. What do you get? $7,180.19.

Do you see how the simple act of investing an additional $200 every year for 20 years has resulted in a much bigger future value? It's almost four times the future value in the original calculation where you didn't invest anything beyond the initial $1,000. And all you had to do was make one deposit of $200 every year for 20 years. This brings us back again to the time value of money. Time (number of periods) can grow money, but the rate of growth is also dependent on the size of your ROI and the size of your principal. In the same way that a higher ROI and a higher number of periods lead to a higher future value, so does a higher principal. Why? Because the $200 you added every year increased the size of your principal, which in turn was subject to that 3% ROI. And because the increasingly larger principal is accruing interest and then accruing more interest on top of that, your investment will grow much larger. That brings us back to a now-familiar concept—compound interest.

So now that we've covered fundamental financial concepts, let's delve further to see how we can apply these concepts to some potentially more profitable investments.

CHAPTER 2

APPLYING BASIC FINANCIAL CONCEPTS

Now that you understand the time value of money (TVM), it's time to see all the instances in which we can use it.

In the previous chapter, we saw how TVM applies to money earning interest in a bank account. Now let's look at different bank-related financial products.

Savings Accounts

You should be familiar with savings accounts. Every bank offers them, and they're a great way to make your money grow over time—which is exactly where TVM comes in. Let's start with an example.

Say your bank is offering a savings account with 2.5% annual interest. If you invest $500 right now and let it accrue interest over 30 years, how much would you have after 30 years? Remember, your $500 is your present value (PV) or starting principal, 2.5% is your interest (ROI), and your time period (N) is 30 years.

Type in the relevant values on your financial calculator. Did you get $1,048.78 for your future value? That means investing $500 once and letting it accrue 2.5% interest annually will result in $1,048.78 after 30 years. And if you subtract your initial $500 from that number, you'll see that your total interest earned was $548.78 ($1,048.78 − $500), which is more than the $500 you started with.

And just to prove the power of TVM, let's assume you invest the $500 in the same savings account paying 2.5% annual interest. But this time, pretend you only keep the money there for 10 years. Plugging in the values should result in a future value of $640.04. And even though you earned $140.04 in interest over 10 years ($640.04 − $500), the amount of interest earned is much smaller than in the previous example. And why is that? Because in the first example, you invested for 30 years, not 10 years. Remember the power of TVM: The longer you invest your money, the more it will grow.

Certificates of Deposit (CDs)

Another popular savings vehicle offered by banks is what's known as a certificate of deposit (CD). A certificate of deposit works like this: You put your money in the CD for a specific amount of time, and in return, the bank will pay you a fixed interest rate (called an APR or Annual Percentage Rate) on the money you gave them. In fact, the interest rates on CDs are quite a bit higher than interest rates on savings accounts or regular bank accounts. And better yet, CDs in the United States are insured by the FDIC (Federal Deposit Insurance Corporation) for up to $250,000, which means your money is guaranteed by the federal government in case the bank somehow loses your money.

This sounds like a great deal. So what's the catch? For one thing, CDs have term lengths and maturity dates so you can't just take your money out anytime you want to, unlike bank accounts or savings accounts. Let's look at an example.

Pretend your bank offers a CD with a 1.5% fixed interest rate and a term length of one year. It also has a required minimum deposit of $1,000. Even though you could deposit more than $1,000, let's say you only deposit $1,000 into this CD. Since it pays an interest rate of 1.5%, you will have $1,015 at the end of one year (the maturity date). That's because $1,000 × 1.015 = $1,015.

So how does the time value of money relate to CDs? Through something known as the Annual Percentage Yield (APY). Here's an example: Let's say your bank offers a CD with a term length of five years and an annual percentage rate (APR) of 3%, compounded semiannually (twice per year). Assume you deposit the minimum amount of $4,000. With this CD, your $4,000 will earn 1.5% interest every six months (3% annual percentage rate divided by 2).

So after your first six months, your $4,000 will have grown to $4,060. That's because $4,000 × 1.015 = $4,060. But here's where it gets even better. Can you guess the amount of interest you'll earn after six more months? If you said another $60, which would bring your total up to $4,120, then you're wrong.

That's because the $4,060 ($4,000 principal + $60 interest) will be subject to the 1.5% rate again. Since $4,060 × 1.015 = $4,120.90, you've made 90 cents more than you would have otherwise. And when interest is applied to your principal and the previously accrued interest, what is that called? That's right—compound interest.

Now let's look at how much this CD would end up being worth after five years thanks to the power of TVM and compound interest. Using your financial calculator, enter 10 for N, or the number of periods (because there are 10 six-month periods across five years), $4,000 for the present value (PV), 1.5 for INT or the interest (because the annual 3% rate is 1.5% per six months), and 0 for the payment (PMT). Now click Calculate or future value (FV). So after five years, your $4,000 earning 1.5% interest every six months will have compounded into the grand total of $4,642.16 (Figure 4: Note that values are rounded up or down to the nearest dollar).

But what if it hadn't compounded all those times? Then your $4,000 would only be earning $60 every six months instead of compounding, which would result in a total of $4,600 ($60 per period × 10 periods added to your $4,000). Through the power of compounding, you've made an extra $42.16, because $4,642.16 − $4,600 = $42.16.

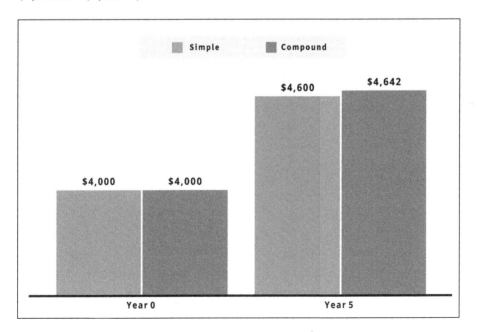

Figure 4

Now, that all sounds great. But what if, after you deposited the money, you had an emergency and needed to get your hands on it? Well, one of the rules of CDs is that you're not supposed to withdraw any of the money until the maturity date. But if you choose to withdraw the money early, you will be assessed a penalty, usually a percentage of your accrued interest. So if you ever need to withdraw that money, make sure the lost interest is worth it.

TVM for Stocks, Bonds, Mutual Funds, and ETFs

Stocks, bonds, mutual funds and ETFs (exchange-traded funds) also utilize the time value of money. We will go into great detail about all four categories in upcoming chapters, but for right now, let's look at how TVM applies to them as well.

First, let's look at stocks, mutual funds, and ETFs. All three are different forms of equity, which is defined as ownership in a company. When you buy shares of stock in a certain company, you now have equity because you own a small piece of the company. The more shares you own, the bigger your ownership stake in the company. If you bought all the shares, you would own the entire company outright.

Mutual funds and ETFs are collections of stocks from different companies, as opposed to a single company's stock. They are often organized by specific criteria, such as an industry (like energy), geography (like Europe), or investment objective (like high-growth or dividends). Although mutual funds and ETFs can also be comprised of only bonds or a combination of stocks and bonds, this specific section deals with equity mutual funds and equity ETFs that only contain stocks.

Now, pretend that you own 100 shares in a particular stock, mutual fund, or ETF. Since all three are types of equity, TVM applies in the same way to all of them. Now, say you bought your 100 shares for $5,000 total, meaning each share was worth $50 (because $5,000/100 = $50). So $5,000 is your present value or starting principal, right? Now pretend that you keep that $5,000 invested for 7 years, and the shares go up in value by 4% every year. Also assume that you don't invest any additional money.

Using your financial calculator, enter 5,000 for your present value or starting principal, 7 for your number of periods, 4 for your interest or rate of return, and 0 for your additional payments or PMT. Now select future value or Calculate. You should see $6,579.66 for your future value. So you've made a profit of $1,579.66, because $6,579.66 − $5,000 = $1,579.66.

So how did TVM help us here? If you divide 1,579.66 by 5,000, you should get 0.3159, or a total return of 31.59%. Remember how our annual rate of return was 4%? If the 4% growth we had every year wasn't compounded, then we'd only have a profit of 28%, because 4 × 7 = 28. But since the returns compounded every year for seven years, our profit was 31.59%.

And since the key word in TVM is "time," let's assume that you invested the same $5,000 for 20 years instead. Enter 5,000 for your present value or starting principal, 4 for your interest or rate of return, 20 for your number of periods, and 0 for your payment or PMT. Now what is your future value? It's $10,955.62. So you made a profit of $5,955.62, because $10,955.62 − $5,000 = $5,955.62.

Do you see how investing for 20 years instead of 7 years made such a big difference? In fact, your profit of $5,955.62 is higher than your initial principal of $5,000. When we divide $5,955.62 by the initial $5,000, we get 1.19. That means you made a profit of 119%. You've more than doubled your money because you invested for a longer period of time, even though it was the same $5,000 and the same 4% annual return.

Go ahead and run the same calculation again, but enter 30 years for your number of periods. Then run another calculation, but with 40 years as your number of periods. Do you see how your net profits keep dwarfing your starting principal of $5,000 (Figure 5: Note that values are rounded up or down to the nearest dollar)? And how more and more of your investment's total value comes from your net profits instead of your starting principal? That's the power of time. It's made your money more valuable. Given enough time, the interest or profits from your investments will be worth far more than the amount of money you initially saved and invested.

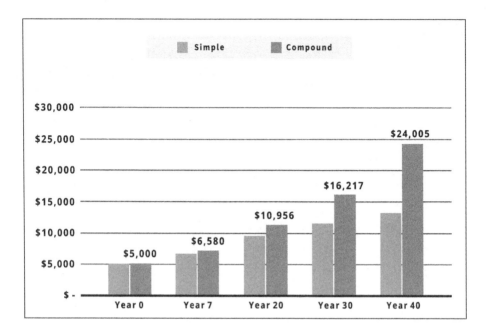

Figure 5

Bonds, in some cases, also utilize the time value of money. A bond is a debt instrument sold to investors, where a government or company that needs money (the borrowers) sells the bonds to investors (the lenders). In exchange for the investors lending them money when they bought the bonds, the government or company pays the investors a (usually) fixed rate of interest as long as they don't sell the bond. When the bond reaches its maturity date, the investor receives his or her initial investment from when they bought the bond. This is in addition to the interest they received every year that they held the bond.

However, the interest you earn from a single bond, in and of itself, is not able to compound through the time value of money. You simply receive the interest payments that you were promised on a regular schedule (like every quarter or once a year). But there is a way you can compound interest from bonds: through a bond mutual fund. A bond mutual fund (also called a bond fund or fixed-income fund) is similar to a stock mutual fund, except it contains a wide variety of bonds rather than stocks. The bonds contained within the bond mutual fund will earn interest every month, and you can choose to reinvest that interest into the fund instead of receiving the money in your bank account.

Here's an example. Say you invest $3,000 into a bond mutual fund that pays 2% interest per year. Since bond mutual funds pay interest monthly, divide 2 by 12 to get 0.1666%, which is the monthly interest rate. Assume that you don't sell the fund for eight years and you don't invest any additional money beyond the interest you earn. Now enter 3,000 for your present value or starting principal, .1666 for your interest or rate of return, 96 for your number of periods or N (because 8 years × 12 months per year = 96 months), and 0 for your payment or PMT. Your bond mutual fund's value after 8 years should be $3,519.84. If the money hadn't compounded every month, you would have a smaller total of $3,479.81, because $3,000 × 0.001666 × 96 = $479.81, which you would add to your initial $3,000.

Now it's time to dive into the wide world of stocks.

CHAPTER 3

STOCKS

You're probably reading this book on your smartphone, tablet, or e-reader. And there's a very good chance your device of choice was made by Apple, Google, or Amazon. And aside from being three of the biggest companies on Earth, each worth hundreds of billions of dollars, what else do they have in common?

They are all publicly traded companies that you can buy stock in. That means you could be an owner of Apple, Google, or Amazon, and you could reap the benefits of your investment as more and more people buy their products and services.

There are two very broad categories of companies: publicly traded and privately owned. A privately owned company is, for the most part, your average small business, like a local café. Often these companies are solely owned by one person, or maybe by a few people such as business partners or private investors. Of course, there are some very large companies worth billions that are privately owned. But for the most part, privately owned companies tend to be what you think of as a typical small business.

When you walk or drive past businesses in your town, you'll see these small businesses side by side with big chain establishments like McDonald's, Starbucks, or Walmart. But the one thing big businesses have that small businesses don't is that they are publicly traded, which means you can buy part of the business anytime you want and become an owner.

Have you ever watched CNBC or other news shows where they mention the stock market? Did it all seem too complicated? Well, don't worry. It's much easier to understand than you think. Simply put, when you buy shares of a publicly traded company's stock, you are buying partial ownership of the company. You are now one of many shareholders in the company. But don't get too excited—even if you owned 10,000 shares of Apple, you wouldn't even own 1% of the company, so you wouldn't be the one in charge making every decision for the company. But your shares would still be worth a few million dollars, which is pretty nice.

So now you understand what a stock is. But there's a lot more to learn. Because buying a stock isn't enough—you must perform your due diligence and research whether or not it's a good investment according to your investment goals and future life plans.

To do this, you'll need to examine various metrics, such as the company's beta and price-to-earnings ratio. Don't worry. Those terms will be defined shortly, along with many others. And in just a few minutes, you'll learn more about stocks than you ever have in your life.

Understanding Stock Terms

Let's step back even further before we get into the details about understanding stocks. Have you ever heard someone say, "The market did really well today" or "There was a downturn in the market"? Well, what exactly is the *market*? The *market* is a broad reference to the Standard & Poor's 500 (or S&P 500). The S&P 500 is a diversified collection of the 500 biggest publicly traded companies in America. They measure the size of these companies by market capitalization (or market cap).

Market capitalization is calculated by multiplying the price per share times the outstanding number of shares.

Company XYZ
48.17
+1.17 (+2.50%)

Previous Close	$47
Open	$47.28
Day's Range	$47.28 – $49.03
52-Week Range	$33.72 – $52.16
Volume	8,235,761
Average Volume	2,739,032
Market Cap	4.7B
Beta	0.70
Price/Earnings Ratio (PE)	23.94
Earnings per Share (EPS)	3.78
Dividend (and Yield)	2.61 (5.5%)
Ex-Dividend Date	2018-11-01
1-Year Target Estimate	$51.23

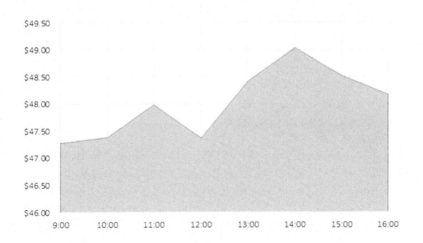

Figure 6

In Figure 6, we see the information for Company XYZ. Do you see where it says the market cap is $4.7 billion? We find that figure by multiplying the price per share times the number of **outstanding shares,** which are shares of a company's stock that are issued or available. So, to find the number of outstanding shares, we divide the market cap by the price per share: $4,700,000,000 divided by $48.17 equals roughly 97,571,102 shares. And if we multiply 97,571,102 shares × $48.17 per share, what do we get? $4,700,000,000, which is the market cap.

When determining how valuable or "big" a publicly traded company is, its market cap is the best indicator.

Note: A higher price per share does not mean that a company has a bigger market cap than a company with a lower price per share. New investors often mistake the share price for the value of the company, which it is not. The share price is simply a measurement of how much money you need to pay to own one single share of the company. Since companies can issue as many or as few shares as they want, the price per share tells you nothing about the value of a company unless you also know how many outstanding shares the company has.

Here's an example: If Company A has a price per share of $22 with 100 million outstanding shares and Company B has a price per share of $78 with 5 million outstanding shares, which company is bigger?

The answer is Company A. That's because its market cap is $2.2 billion ($22 per share × 100,000,000 outstanding shares). Company B may have a higher price per share at $78, but its market cap is only $390 million ($78 per share × 5,000,000 outstanding shares). Do you see why price per share alone is *not* a good indicator of a company's size?

Let's go back to Figure 6 and examine some more terms. **Previous close** refers to the closing price of the stock on the previous trading day (Monday through Friday). **Open** refers to the price the stock opened at today. Note that there can be a big gap between the day's previous close and today's opening price. That's because company-specific events, such as quarterly earnings reports, may be released before the trading day begins. If earnings are good, the opening price will be several points higher than the previous closing price (because investors will no longer be willing to sell shares as cheaply as they would have the day before). If earnings turned out to be lower than expected, the opening price will be several points lower (because buyers will no longer be willing to pay as much as they would have the previous day). How much the stock rises or falls is not an exact science, but just remember that stocks react to news much like people do. There could also be a significant economic event that affects the market as a whole, either positively (like a falling unemployment rate) or negatively (like a major terrorist attack).

Day's range is the price range that the stock traded in that day. It contains the high and low price for the day.

52-week range refers to the stock's lowest and highest price within the last 52 weeks, or one year.

Volume refers to the number of shares that were traded (bought and sold) that day. Average volume refers to the average number of shares normally traded each day for that particular stock.

Here's a pop quiz for you. If a stock is trading at a very high volume, is that a good thing? The answer is: it depends. In Figure 6, we see that the volume for that particular day (8,235,761 shares) is about three times the average volume (2,739,032 shares) for Company XYZ's stock. On this day, Company XYZ's stock ended up 1.17 points higher, or a 2.50% increase. In other words, roughly three times as many investors as usual bought shares of Company XYZ today, which sent the stock price soaring.

Company M
109.85
-5.37 (-4.70%)

Previous Close	**$115.22**
Open	**$113.45**
Day's Range	**$107.82-$114.13**
52-Week Range	**$58.92-$122.56**
Volume	**13,675,756**
Average Volume	**1,598,932**
Market Cap	**13.7B**
Beta	**1.40**
Price/Earnings Ratio (PE)	**198.66**
Earnings per Share (EPS)	**0.58**
Dividend (and Yield)	**N/A**
Ex-Dividend Date	**N/A**
1-Year Target Estimate	**$105.36**

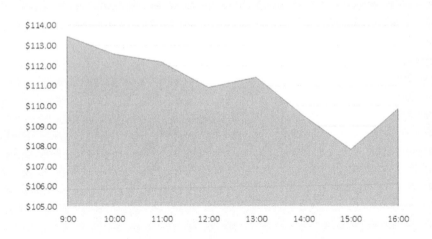

Figure 7

Can high trading volume also be a bad sign? Yes!

In Figure 7, we see that the stock for Company M, a technology company, had a trading volume of over 13.6 million shares—roughly nine times the average daily volume. But check out the price. Company M dropped 5.37 points, losing 4.70% of its value in just one day. That's because its extremely high volume was due to so many investors selling the stock. This is the opposite of what happened in the previous example with Company XYZ.

Beta

In Figures 6 and 7, do you see the word beta? **Beta** refers to a stock's volatility in relation to the market. Remember how the S&P 500 represents the market as a whole? Well, a stock's beta is a great way to gauge how a specific stock will move compared to the S&P 500.

In Figure 6, we see that Company XYZ has a beta of 0.70. What does this mean? It means that Company XYZ's stock will generally underperform the S&P 500 by 30% if the S&P goes up and will over-perform the S&P 500 by 30% if the S&P goes down. For example, if the S&P 500's price moves up by 2%, then Company XYZ will move up by 1.4% on average, because 70% of 2% = 1.4%. And if the S&P 500 moves down by 2%, Company XYZ will only move down by 1.4% on average. In other words, because Company XYZ has a beta of less than 1, it is considered less volatile than the market as a whole because the S&P 500 has a beta of exactly 1.

What about stocks with betas higher than 1? Let's look at Company M in Figure 7 again. It has a beta of 1.4. What does this mean? It means Company M is 40% more volatile than the S&P 500. So if the S&P 500 moved up by 2%, Company M would move up by 2.8% on average (because 2 × 1.4 = 2.8). And if the S&P 500 moved down by 2%, then Company M would move down by 2.8% on average (again, because 2 × 1.4 = 2.8). Keep in mind that the beta-related move of a stock's price assumes all other things are equal. So, the stock may make larger or smaller moves that are not completely related to beta.

Note: Beta is never a guarantee of how a stock will perform in the future. It's a mathematical tool stock analysts use to help understand how risky or safe a particular stock tends to be on average. It is always possible for any stock, regardless of its beta, to drop to zero and for you to lose your entire investment.

What makes certain stocks have low betas and others have high betas? That depends on various factors, but the particular sector a company belongs to is a major factor. A fast-food restaurant like McDonald's is part of the **consumer discretionary sector**. This sector deals with companies that sell items that people often buy but that are not truly essential. Whenever you buy fast food or something from Amazon, that's part of this sector. You may not need a Big Mac or the latest John Grisham novel, but you definitely want them.

This is different from the **consumer staples sector**, which features companies that sell essential products like laundry detergent, toothpaste, and toilet paper. Such companies, like Procter & Gamble, tend to have betas of less than 1. People will still buy these essential products regardless of how the economy is doing. Therefore, companies in this sector are less volatile than the market and can often withstand downturns in the market better than stocks with higher betas.

On the other hand, Company M has a higher beta for several reasons. For one, it's part of the **technology sector**. Tech companies spend billions of dollars in research and development because it's a highly competitive industry. Their products are also far more expensive than a Big Mac, so consumers demand the very best. Tech companies like Apple and Google tend to have higher betas than the S&P 500.

Earnings Per Share (EPS)

Now we come to **earnings per share (EPS)**. This is another valuable metric to use when determining whether to buy a stock. It's calculated by dividing the earnings by the number of outstanding shares.

What are earnings? They are the company's bottom line: the net profit the company makes after interest, taxes, depreciation, and amortization. Earnings are the same as **net income**, which is the last line on an income statement, which will be discussed in the next chapter.

If a stock has an EPS of $2, then that means $2 of every share's price comes from earnings. So if the stock is priced at $40 per share, that means it's trading at 20 times its earnings (20 × $2 = $40). Think of the non-earnings portion of a share of stock—in this case, $38 (because $40 − $2 = $38). So that extra $38 investors are paying is a sort of premium. They pay 20 times the company's actual earnings because that's how much they value it.

Usually, the higher a company's EPS is, the better. That means the company can take those earnings (profits) and reinvest them into the company, which will generate even bigger profits for shareholders in the future (because the stock goes up), or they can use some of those earnings to pay dividends.

Dividends

When companies earn money, they have to decide what to do with it. Often, they will invest that money back into the business in new projects or products to help the company grow even faster. Sometimes though, companies earn far more money than they actually need to maintain and grow the business. In those cases, companies may pay out the extra cash from earnings as dividends to investors.

A **dividend** is a specific amount of money that some companies pay to investors every quarter for holding the stock. Companies pay dividends because they think the best thing for the owners of the stock is to use the cash instead of the company using that cash for something else. That's right, they pay you to own the stock.

Keep in mind that not all companies pay dividends. For example, newly established companies often won't pay dividends because they want to use that cash to invest further in the business. Since dividends are openly declared by companies, they are obligated to set aside money to pay them every quarter. New companies are not going to place that burden on themselves, even if they are generating huge profits, because they need to invest their profits back into the company so they can grow even more. And even some very large companies won't pay dividends because they'd prefer to plow the profits back into the company.

Among companies that do tend to pay dividends are utility companies and certain blue chip companies, or those companies that are large, well known, and highly profitable. Some examples of blue chip companies are General Electric and Microsoft. Aside from being massively successful, you have definitely used their products at some point, if not on a daily basis.

To illustrate how dividends work, let's pretend that Company D pays an annual dividend of $1.60 per share. So as long as you own Company D's stock, you will receive 40 cents for every share that you own every three months in the form of a dividend payment. This is because the $1.60 annual dividend is divided by 4 to create the quarterly payments of 40 cents per share. Since there are 12 months in a year, each quarter is three months. So, if you owned 100 shares of Company D, then you'd receive $40 every three months (0.40 × 100 = $40) just for holding the stock. Pretty neat, right?

But there's more. When you receive dividends from a stock, you have two choices. You can either keep the money and put it in your bank account, or you can enroll in a Dividend Reinvestment Program (DRIP). If you choose to do that, then the dividends you earn are automatically used to buy more shares of the stock. If you don't have a plan for what to do with your quarterly dividend payments, you should probably enroll in a DRIP so that you can continue to compound your investments and benefit from TVM.

Remember how you were getting paid $40 per quarter through Company D's stock dividends? If you enroll in the DRIP program, that $40 will be used to buy additional shares in Company D. But here's something to ponder: If Company D is currently trading at $100 per share, and you're reinvesting $40 every quarter through the DRIP program, that means you'll receive an additional 0.4 shares every quarter (because $40/$100 = 0.4). How is this possible? It's because in the DRIP program, your dividends can purchase fractions of shares.

Keep in mind that stock prices change daily, so if Company D's stock was lower than $100 in the following quarter, your reinvested dividends would pay for more shares than before. Of course, the stock itself is worth less than before, so that's not necessarily a good thing. And if the share price is higher than $100, your reinvested dividends would pay for fewer additional shares. But the stock would be worth more, so that's the positive trade-off.

A term that's used when discussing dividends is **yield**. The yield of a dividend-paying stock indicates the size of the dividend relative to the share price. It's a great way to tell if a dividend-paying stock is worth buying. To find the yield, simply take the annual dividend per share and divide it by the stock's current price per share. Just to keep it simple, we'll use round numbers. Let's say that Verizon's stock is currently selling for $100 per share and pays an annual dividend of $3.00 per share, or 75 cents per quarter (because $3/4 = 0.75). Verizon's yield would then be 3%. That's because $3/$100 = 3%.

What does this mean? Well, the higher a dividend-paying stock's yield is, the better value it is. That's because you're getting paid more for owning the stock relative to the share price. To put it another way, which kind of bank account would you rather have? One that paid 1% interest or one that paid 3% interest? You'd choose 3%, right? Because the bank is willing to pay you 3% of all the money in your account if you keep it with them instead of paying you just 1% of the money in your account. In the same way, a high-yield stock pays you more money in dividends relative to what the stock is selling for than a stock with a lower yield would.

Keep in mind that some lower-yield stocks may pay you more dividends in absolute dollars, but that doesn't mean it's a better value. For example, if Company A pays $3 in annual dividends per share and has a yield of 1%, and Company B pays $1 in annual dividends per share and has a yield of 5%, which is the better value? The answer is Company B, because of its higher yield. Since the yield is 5% and the annual dividend is $1 per share, that means the price per share is $20, because $1/0.05 = $20. Since the yield is 5%, you're basically getting a 5% discount on the stock because they're paying you 5% of your total investment in the stock just for owning it. Contrast that with Company A, where the 1% yield means you're only getting a 1% discount.

Let's say you owned 100 shares of Company B at $20 per share, which means you'd have $2,000 worth of stock. Since the yield is 5%, you'd receive $100 in annual dividends (because $2,000 × 5% = $100), or $25 every quarter. If you take the $100 in dividends you received and subtract it from the $2,000 that you paid for the stock, you really paid $1,900 for the stock, a savings of $100. Since that $100 savings is 5% of $2,000, you have received a discount of 5%, which is the same amount as the yield. Make sense?

Now we're down to the last two terms shown on most stock charts: the ex-dividend date and the 1-year target estimate. Since we were just talking about dividends, let's talk about the **ex-dividend date**. This is the deadline for receiving the next quarter's dividends. If Company A's ex-dividend date is March 31, and they announce the dividend to be paid in the next quarter (three months later) is $1 per share, you must own the stock before March 31 in order to receive the next dividend of $1 per share. If you buy the stock on or after March 31, you will not receive that dividend in the next quarter.

The **1-year target estimate** is the stock price that various analysts predict will be reached within one year. This estimate is based on numerous factors such as earnings, growth potential, industry competitors, and more. The estimate is also not an exact science. However, it is an educated guess reached by financial experts, so it's a potential indicator of where the stock may be headed within the next year.

Price/Earnings (PE) Ratio

Now we come to the **PE ratio**, or price/earnings ratio. It's a great way to tell if a stock is overvalued or undervalued. In other words, whether a stock is a good "bang for the buck." Simply put, the PE ratio is how much investors are willing to pay for each dollar of a company's earnings. The PE ratio is calculated by dividing the price per share by the company's earnings per share.

A good PE ratio (meaning the stock is undervalued) is as low as possible. A bad PE ratio (meaning the stock is overvalued) is as high as possible. To illustrate this concept in basic terms, let's use round numbers.

Pretend that Company X has a PE ratio of 30. That means investors are willing to pay 30 times every $1 of a company's earnings to own the stock. If Company X had earnings per share of $2, then one share of Company X's stock is selling for $60 because 30 × $2 = $60. Simple, right?

Generally speaking, a PE ratio of less than 10 means the stock is undervalued, and a PE ratio of 20 or more means the stock is overvalued. But this is not a hard-and-fast rule at all. Some PE ratios may be very high for different reasons, and those stocks may still be a good investment. Likewise, it's possible for a very poorly run company to have a low PE ratio, like 5, and still be a terrible investment because the company may go out of business soon. The PE ratio is an indicator of where investors think a stock is going. Investors are willing to pay higher prices for companies they expect to grow a lot, so high-growth companies tend to have higher PE ratios.

Let's look at the information in Figure 7 for Company M's stock. Do you see its PE ratio? It's 198.66. Based solely on what I just told you about PE ratios, you might think that Company M is not a good stock to buy, right? Wrong. That's because PE ratios do not exist in a bubble. They are a useful tool, but they should not be the only tool.

So here's another pop quiz for you. Pretend Company M is a new technology company that makes virtual reality video games. The PE ratio for Company M does not deter investors because they may think that virtual reality video games are the next big thing in the technology industry. In other words, investors are willing to pay almost 200 times Company M's actual earnings per share to buy one share of their stock. That means investors expect the company's earnings to grow rapidly over the next few years. So in this particular case, PE ratio is not the best metric to use.

Now that you understand all the basic terms involving stocks, it's time to dive into stock analysis.

CHAPTER 4

FUNDAMENTAL ANALYSIS VERSUS TECHNICAL ANALYSIS

It's time to delve deeper into the world of investing in stocks. You must study stocks to determine which are potentially great investments and which are likely to underperform.

To see why it's so important to pick stocks wisely, let's look at the numbers. Imagine you could invest $10,000 in each of three stocks, and you're magically able to predict their performance. Stock A will give you a 5% return every year, Stock B will give you a 10% return, and Stock C will give you a 15% return.

When you run the numbers in a financial calculator over a 20-year period, here's how much money you'll have after 20 years:

Stock A (5%): $26,532.98

Stock B (10%): $67,275.00

Stock C (15%): $163,665.37

As you can see, earning a higher ROI with your investments could mean the difference between retiring with a small nest egg and retiring with a much larger one. The difference between picking a mediocre stock like Stock A and a great stock like Stock C is astronomical over 20 or more years of investing.

The Power of Zero

There's another rule you should understand about investing, which is the power of 0. Let's say you invest $1,000 in a stock and the company goes bankrupt. Your shares are now worth $0. How much of an ROI do you need to earn back the money you lost?

The answer is: you can't! Once you hit 0, even the greatest investment in the world won't make up for it.

This is why you have to diversify your investments. Never put all your money into one stock, bond, or investment, because if you lose it—you're out! You lost all of your principal, which means you'll have to start over from 0.

So even though you're aiming to pick stocks with high returns if you can find them, you never want to put all your money into one investment. Furthermore, you should never fool yourself into thinking that you know, for sure, that an investment will be a good one. Even professional stock pickers and investors are wrong much of the time.

So always be wary of the power of 0, and diversify your investments. That means owning multiple stocks, bonds, or other investment vehicles so that you won't lose most or all of your investment portfolio if something bad happens.

With that said, let's jump into stock analysis.

How to Analyze Stocks

When it comes to analyzing stock investments, there are two major schools of thought: fundamental analysis and technical analysis. While both categories have their pros and cons, the truth is that they work best together, not separately.

Fundamental Analysis

Let's look at fundamental analysis first. **Fundamental analysis involves analyzing a company's financial statements as well as its competitors, industry, and the general economic environment.** The goal of fundamental analysis is to assess how well a company is doing financially, and how likely they are to continue to grow and increase their profits.

Every company has three financial statements: a balance sheet, an income statement, and a statement of cash flows. Since this is a book on investing and not accounting, we won't go into too much detail about the content in those statements. But let's acquire a basic understanding of what they are, because only then will the field of investing start to make sense.

Balance Sheet

A balance sheet is a type of financial statement that lists a company's assets and liabilities at a given point in time. In case you didn't know, **an asset is something a company owns that can be used to generate profits**.

A liability is something that is owed by a company, such as when a company is required to pay back a loan or when a vendor sends a company a shipment of product and sends an invoice for the amount owed to pay for it. When you need to know the size of a company's assets, which indicate its financial health, there's a simple equation for that: Assets = Liabilities + Owner's Equity.

Owner's equity is defined as the owner's financial investment in the business. From that, we subtract any withdrawals he or she takes, then add the net income (or, if the company is doing poorly, subtract the net loss) since the start of the business. But when you purchase stock in a company, you own a small piece of the company. Therefore, when dealing with a publicly traded company, owner's equity is better defined as shareholders' equity. Just like liabilities, owner's equity is a claim on a company's assets.

Let's look at the equation again. Imagine that Company ABC has $1,000,000 in assets. Now assume that they have $300,000 in liabilities and $700,000 in owner's equity. If you add $300,000 and $700,000, what do you get? $1,000,000. Remember, both sides of this equation must always balance because: Assets = Liabilities + Owner's Equity. And in this case, $1,000,000 = $300,000 + $700,000.

Income Statement

The next type of major financial statement is the income statement. It is released quarterly (every three months) and is often compared with income statements from previous quarters or years to determine how well a company is doing. It is also known as a profit and loss (P&L) statement because **it involves calculating all sources of revenue (money received from the company's sales) and subtracting the expenses (such as employees' wages and rent) to find the company's profit.**

At the bottom of an income statement is the company's net income (net profit), which is the company's earnings after interest, taxes, depreciation, and amortization. Remember, **the higher a company's net income, the better**.

Statement of Cash Flows

Finally, we come to the statement of cash flows, also known as the cash flow statement or CFS. **A company's CFS keeps track of the cash that goes in and out of the company**. There are three cash flow categories within a CFS: Operations, Investing, and Financing.

Cash flow from Operations refers to cash the company receives from their business operations. This is the same number indicated by net income on the income statement. Cash flow from Operations deals with money earned by the company through their normal business activities such as selling their products. They do not include things like investing in new factories because while the factories may be used to manufacture the company's products, the factories themselves are not being sold by the company to their customers.

Cash flow from Investing involves the company's use of cash to invest in the company itself. So the money spent to build those factories? They would fall under this category. And since money is being spent, this would be a cash outflow because money is leaving the company. But Cash flow from Investing can also lead to a positive cash inflow. If a publicly traded company sells shares of stock to investors, the money they receive is a positive cash flow. They can then use that money to invest in the company further.

Cash flow from Financing is the final category. This involves cash used for any of the company's financing activities. Going back to the factory example, let's pretend that instead of paying cash outright for the factory, the company decides to borrow the money. If they borrow $500,000 to build the factory, they now owe that $500,000 to their creditor (the person or bank loaning them money). So, if they had to pay back this debt to the tune of $10,000 a month, then $10,000 would be subtracted from the company's cash on hand every month.

The important thing to remember: the higher a company's positive cash flow, the better. Here's an example. Let's say that your monthly net income (after taxes) is $2,000. Your rent is $800, you have no credit card debt, and all your bills add up to $500. So you have $2,000 in cash and pay out a total of $1,300 ($800 + $500) in expenses. That leaves you with $700 in the bank every month. That means you have a positive cash flow of $700.

Now pretend that you still net $2,000 a month but you pay $1,200 in rent, $700 in bills, and you pay off $200 in credit card debt every month. So you owe $2,100 in rent, bills and credit card debt ($1,200 + $700 + $200) but only have $2,000 to pay it off. That leaves you with -$100 (negative $100) in the bank every month. That means you have a negative cash flow of $100.

Which financial situation is better? Obviously, it's the first one. When a person runs out of cash, they might have to declare bankruptcy. Likewise, when a company runs out of cash, it might have to declare bankruptcy. However, unlike people, when a company declares bankruptcy, that company will often cease to exist. That's why having a positive cash flow is so important for a company because companies that don't manage their cash flow well go out of business.

Keep in mind that it is possible for companies to show huge profits on their income statement and still go bankrupt (Enron is a great example). And, just like with Enron, it's possible for companies to "cook their books" by lying about how much money they're actually earning or how much cash they actually have. Although this kind of financial fraud is rare, it does happen, and it's another reason why you should diversify your investments.

Analyzing a Company

Now let's show how this works in a practical application. Instead of doing a deep dive into various numbers, let's simplify fundamental analysis as much as possible. Assume you find a particular stock that has excellent metrics: a beta equal to or less than 1, a PE ratio of less than 20, an increasing dividend with a high yield, increasing positive cash flow, and optimistic sentiments by various analysts. By these standards, fundamental analysis would tell you that this stock is a good buy.

Now let's look at this company's competitors. Is this company the most successful within its industry? Or is it the least successful, or perhaps somewhere in the middle of the pack? If it's the most successful, that's another reason to invest in it. In business, there tends to be just a few big winners in each industry, and the biggest winners tend to earn the majority of the profits. If it's not the most successful company in its industry, then perhaps you can look at its more successful competitors and examine their metrics and financial statements to find out if they are better choices. Unless there's a darn good reason for it, you should be very cautious about investing in smaller companies in an industry that's dominated by much larger competitors.

Let's assume you're analyzing a company that is the most successful in the industry and has the positive metrics to go along with it. What about the general economic climate? How will that affect this particular stock? If the economy is doing well, then all the more reason to invest in this particular stock. But if the economy is doing poorly or is close to entering a recession, this stock may not be a good investment right now.

That could depend on various factors. For example, is your stock part of the financial services industry? If the economy falls into a recession, financial services stocks (such as JP Morgan or Citigroup) will certainly fall more than most other types of stocks because their performance depends on a healthy economy. So, these would not be good investments in a bad economic climate.

In this scenario, you could go with defensive stocks. These are stocks that are "recession-proof." In a bad economy, they will fall just like other stocks but not by nearly as much because they are part of the consumer staples sector mentioned previously. People will still buy their products (toilet paper, soap, toothpaste, etc.) because they are basic items everyone uses. In contrast, stocks in the consumer discretionary sector would fall by more because those involve products and services that are wanted but not truly needed (eating out at restaurants, buying things on Amazon, etc.).

Fundamental analysis involves four basic factors: a company's financial statements, their competitors, their industry, and the general economic climate. The better you understand these four components of investing, the better investment decisions you'll be able to make, and the more likely you are to get a higher ROI when you invest.

Technical Analysis

Technical analysis is a rigorous examination of a stock's price movements. It's used in an attempt to predict how a stock is likely to perform in the near future. Technical analysis essentially uses different metrics to give you a better perspective of buying and selling patterns of other investors in the stock you're analyzing to see what you can learn from their behavior.

Technical analysis is different from fundamental analysis because **technical analysis uses information such as price and volume to analyze securities**. In other words, a technical analyst does not look at a company's financial statements like a fundamental analyst would do. Technical analysis is strictly based on information contained within a stock's chart. These charts are available on any financial website (such as Google Finance), though there are many websites available that specifically deal with technical analysis and provide all the necessary charting tools.

Volume

The most popular technical indicator, and one that can be easily understood, is volume. As you may recall from the chapter on stocks, volume reflects the trading level (amount of shares bought and sold) of a specific stock.

Remember that volume can mean that investors are either buying or selling the stock in large numbers. Technical analysis would use volume to determine a stock's momentum and trend. For example, a stock that is trading at high volume because many investors are buying it would indicate that the trend and momentum are positive, making the stock a good buy based only on technical analysis. And if volume was high because many investors were selling, the stock is likely to keep losing value and you should sell it.

Note: When someone says you "should" buy or sell a stock, always be skeptical and do your own critical thinking and research. You should always ask, "Why?" Saying you should or should not buy a stock is simply an opinion, and they may not have any facts to back it up. Make sure you get the facts, and that you have multiple facts to back up your case before you decide to buy or sell a stock. Technical analysis provides many tools you can use to assess the facts around a stock's price movements, but the best technical traders are the ones who only buy or sell when they have multiple facts to support their decisions.

Moving Averages (MAs)

Another common technical indicator is a security's moving average, or MA. A moving average is a constantly updating average of a stock's value based on a certain timeframe. For example, a 10-day moving average involves adding up the stock's price over the last 10 days and dividing that amount by 10. If a stock's current 10-day MA was higher than its previous 10-day MA (the 10 days before yesterday), that indicates that the price is likely to climb. The opposite is true if the current 10-day MA is lower than its previous 10-day MA.

But what about longer moving averages? They are more helpful because longer moving averages are a more reliable indicator of a stock's price movement over longer periods of time. Technical analysis frequently compares moving averages of different timeframes to try to predict the direction of the stock's price in the near future.

Look at Figure 8. Here we are comparing the 50-day MA and 200-day MA of cosmetics company L'Oréal. In the lower left-hand portion of the chart, we see the 50-day MA cross above the 200-day MA.

Figure 8
Chart courtesy of StockCharts.com

What does this mean? It means that the average price of L'Oréal stock during the last 50 days is higher than its average price over the last 200 days. Now, do you see how the 50-day MA continues to rise above the 200-day MA over the next several months? So at any of those points, the stock's average price within the previous 50 days is higher than the average price within the previous 200 days. The moving average recalculates itself on a daily basis. The 50- and 200-day MAs in April don't refer to the exact same days as the MAs in July because we are at a different point in time now. The average keeps moving with the calendar, hence the name: moving average.

If you look at the chart for L'Oréal, you'll notice that the stock's price rose consistently for a few months after the 50-day MA crossed above the 200-day MA. Do you see the connection? As the 50-day MA rose above the 200-day MA, so did the stock's price. And as the price kept climbing up, so did the 50-day MA, because the price kept climbing up. The more recently and consistently that the stock's price climbed, the higher the 50-day MA moves. Make sense?

When the 50-day MA crosses above the 200-day MA, this is known as a golden cross and is an indicator to technical analysts to purchase the stock (or hold it if they already own it). The opposite of a golden cross is a death cross, which occurs when the 50-day MA crosses below the 200-day MA. We see an example in Figure 9.

Figure 9
Chart courtesy of StockCharts.com

Look at the left side next to the text. Do you see the 50-day MA cross below the 200-day MA? And do you see how the stock's price eventually slips before taking a dive in May? Notice the steep drop in the 50-day MA as that happens. And even after the stock bounces back a bit, it's not enough to move the 50-day MA back up. For a technical analyst, this would be a sign to sell (or not buy the stock if they don't own it).

Trends are very powerful in technical analysis. Just because the 50-day MA crosses above or below the 200-day MA and continues to either skyrocket or plummet, that does not mean the price will always rise or always fall. Falling stock prices could bounce back to an extent, and rising stock prices could fall slightly, but in both cases the trend is moving in the same direction of a climbing price or falling price.

There is far more information to be learned about technical analysis than can be covered in an introductory book like this. *How Technical Analysis Works* by Bruce M. Kamich is an excellent primer on learning more about this very interesting field of stock analysis if you want to learn more.

Combine Your Analysis

It's much better to use technical analysis after you've done your fundamental analysis to identify which stocks or investments are likely to succeed over the long-term. Here's why. Imagine you have Company A, an excellent company that's a leader in the industry and is likely to continue growing quickly. You also have Company B, a small player in the industry that's expected to grow a little bit. Fundamentally, these companies are completely different, and your chances of success with Company A are much higher over the long-term. So even if all the technical analysis tells you to buy Company B right now, you may still be better off buying Company A because, over the long-term, it's likely to be much more profitable.

That's why, if you're a long-term investor, you should do your fundamental analysis first before simply diving into technical analysis.

C H A P T E R 5

BONDS

Have you ever borrowed a few dollars from a friend? What about millions or billions or trillions of dollars? Probably not. But the federal government does it all the time. So do state and municipal governments, as well as publicly traded companies of all sizes. Whenever governments or companies need to borrow a lot of money, they issue bonds to investors.

A bond is a debt instrument that benefits both the borrowers (governments or companies) and lenders (investors). When an investor purchases a bond, they are loaning that money to the issuing government or company. In exchange, the investor receives a specific yield (interest rate) for his trouble. Bonds are also known as fixed-income securities because they pay specific amounts to investors on a regular basis. This is not to be confused with people like senior citizens living on a "fixed income," which usually refers to Social Security.

But let's back up for a second. When we were talking about dividend-paying stocks, the yield referred to the dividend paid per share divided by the price per share. But bonds are slightly different.

Bond yields are calculated by dividing the coupon payment by the bond's price. A **coupon payment** is the amount paid to bond investors (usually semiannually, meaning every six months) for buying the bond in the first place. Because you're loaning money for a certain amount of time, you need to be compensated for your investment. And the amount you are compensated is determined by the interest rate.

Interest rates are a foundation of any modern economy. You've seen them when paying your mortgage, credit card, and loans. They are the cost of borrowing for the borrower. And they are the benefit of lending for the lender. A government or company that needs to borrow money wants the lowest interest rate possible, while a bond investor wants the highest interest rate possible. When the Federal Reserve sets the interest rate, the bond market will react to this information. Bond prices will be affected by changes in interest rates, as I will explain later on.

As in the previous chapter, let's use much smaller round numbers to help illustrate these concepts. Pretend that the government or a company needs to raise $30,000. They borrow $30,000 by issuing bonds. Let's assume they issue 300 bonds priced at $100 each (300 × $100 = $30,000). But since investors need to be compensated, let's say those bonds have a yield of 10%. That means an investor who owns one $100 bond will receive $10 (10% of $100) per year, or $5 every six months, in exchange for loaning the government or company $100 when they bought the bond.

So far, this sounds like a dividend-paying stock, right? Well, not quite. For one, buying a stock means you own a piece of the company. Buying a bond means you are loaning money to a company or government, but you don't own any piece of it. And keep in mind that bonds, whether from a government or a company, all have a **maturity date.** In other words, bonds have an expiration date, whereas stocks do not.

What does this mean? In this example, it means that the investor who paid $100 for one bond will receive that $100 back once the bond reaches the maturity date. And in the meantime, he will receive the coupon payments for every year that he owns the bond. As mentioned before, the coupon payment is the actual dollar amount paid to an investor annually for holding the bond, similar to the actual dividend paid to a stockholder. The yield of a bond is the coupon payment divided by the bond's price (or the cost of the bond). It is similar to the yield when discussing dividend-paying stocks. Keep in mind that the bond's current price may differ from its **face value** (also known as **par value**), which is the amount paid at maturity.

So, in the previous example, the bond's face value is $100 because that's what it pays at maturity. It also happens to be the bond's current price in this example. And an investor who buys the $100 bond is loaning the government or company $100. The $10 the investor receives every year for owning the bond is the coupon payment. Dividing the coupon payment of $10 by the bond's face value of $100 results in a *yield* of 10% ($10/$100 = 10%).

Now let's say the maturity of this specific bond is 30 years. If the investor owns the bond for 30 years, then at the end of Year 30, he will get the $100 back because the bond has matured. He has also received the $10 coupon payment every year for 30 years for a total of $300 ($10 × 30). Add that $300 to the $100 principal he gets back, and he has a grand total of $400 after 30 years from an initial investment of $100. So, since his profit is $300 ($400 − $100), he has made a 300% profit. Not bad, right?

But what if the investor doesn't want to keep the bond for 30 years? Well, he can sell it at any time. But the downside is that once he sells the bond, he no longer receives coupon payments. It's just like how selling a dividend-paying stock means you don't get those dividends anymore.

Bond Ratings

Before purchasing a bond, you need to know whether it's a good investment or not. One way to do that is to check the bond rating. These are set by ratings agencies such as Moody's and Fitch. When it comes to credit ratings, the highest-rated governments and companies are those that are the least likely to default on their debts. They are typically given the highest rating (AAA) or slightly lower (AA or A). Governments and companies that are in poor financial shape and more likely to default (unable to pay their debts) receive lower bond ratings, ranging from BBB, BB or B, all the way down to C or D for the riskiest bonds.

The downside of buying bonds from a highly rated government or company is that the yield will be relatively low. That's because there is little to no risk of default, so the investor does not need to be compensated too much for his trouble. The low yield is a trade-off for the relative safety of the issuing government or company.

By contrast, a government or company with a low bond rating will offer significantly higher yields. That's because investors need to be compensated for the tremendous risk they are taking by purchasing these bonds. The high yield is a trade-off for the relative instability of the issuing government or company. But be very careful when dealing with these governments and companies—if they default on their debt, you could be left with a major loss, or even lose your entire investment.

Now that we've covered the basics of bonds, let's examine the various types of bonds available.

US Government Bonds

The federal government routinely issues trillions of dollars of bonds every year to fund various things such as the military and social programs. Although the government receives trillions of dollars in tax revenue every year, that's not enough to pay for all the government's operations and programs. So, they need to issue bonds (borrow money) to pay for the rest. Investors in America and around the world buy these government bonds, known as Treasuries or Treasury Bonds, because they are the safest debt instruments in the world, backed by the full faith and credit of the United States government. The American government has never defaulted on their Treasuries, so they are especially attractive for investors who don't like risk.

Treasuries vary based on maturity dates, yields, and prices. Treasuries with maturity dates of one year or less are referred to as Treasury Bills or **T-Bills**. Their maturity dates can range from a few days to one month, three months, six months, or one year. These are short-term debt instruments, and as a result, do not have regular coupon payments. Why is that? Because of their very early maturity dates. In other words, since investors only have to hold T-Bills for a very short period of time, the odds of the government defaulting within that time period are extremely low.

Now you might be thinking, "Why should I invest in them if I don't receive coupon payments?" The answer is that you still receive a return on your investment. Instead of receiving coupon payments, an investor who purchases T-Bills receives a discount at the time of purchase. For example, if you buy a T-Bill with a one-year maturity that has a face value of $1,000 (the smallest denomination offered), you will actually buy it at an offered discount price, let's say $950. So instead of receiving coupon payments, when this T-Bill matures after one year, you will receive $1,000. In other words, you spent $950 and received $1,000 one year later for a profit of 5.26%, because $50/$950 = 5.26%. T-Bills are optimal for people who prefer safe, conservative investments and not for people who seek risk or high-growth investments. Another advantage of T-Bills is that while they are subject to federal taxes, they are not subject to state or local taxes.

The next category of Treasuries is Treasury Notes or **T-Notes**. These have maturities ranging from one year to 10 years, and unlike T-Bills, they do have coupon payments that the investor receives twice a year. Like T-Bills, T-Notes are exempt from state and local taxes. But the presence of coupon payments for T-Notes is a major advantage over T-Bills.

The final category of Treasuries is Treasury Bonds or **T-Bonds**. A T-Bond is similar to a T-Note, except that a T-Bond's maturity is anywhere from 10 to 30 years. T-Bonds are also taxable at the federal level, just like T-Notes and T-Bills.

Now here's a pop quiz for you. Aside from the opportunity to receive more coupon payments due to their longer maturities, is there any other advantage to owning a T-Bond over a T-Note or T-Bill? The answer is yes.

Bond Maturity and Interest Rates

The maturity of a bond and the interest rate assigned to it are directly related. In most cases, the longer the maturity of a bond, the higher the interest rate (coupon payments) that the investor receives. Why is that? I'll illustrate with a few simple examples:

Let's say I can borrow $1,000 from you and that I will pay you back in one year. That means that you'll go a whole year without that $1,000 in your bank account. So, I have to compensate you for it, right? But since you'll get your money back in only a year, I wouldn't have to compensate you too much, so let's assume you charge me a 2% interest rate paid semiannually. Two percent of $1,000 is $20, so that means I will pay you $10 every six months for a total of $20 by the end of the year, at which point you will also get back your $1,000. You made a 2% profit because $20/$1,000 = 2%.

Now imagine I want to borrow $1,000 and that I'll pay you back in 10 years. That's a long time to go without $1,000, so you charge me a higher interest rate for the inconvenience of having to wait so long to get paid back. Let's say you charge me a 5% interest rate paid semiannually. Five percent of $1,000 is $50, so that means I will pay you $25 every six months ($50 annually) for 10 years straight. At the end of Year 10, I will also pay you back your $1,000. So, I paid you a total of $500 ($50 × 10) over 10 years and your initial $1,000 principal. You now have $1,500 and have made a profit of $500, or 50% (because $500/$1,000 = 50%).

Now imagine I want to borrow $1,000 and I'll pay you back in 30 years. That's a really long time to go without that money, isn't it? Let's assume you charge me an interest rate of 10% paid semiannually for the inconvenience. Since 10% of $1,000 is $100, I will pay you $50 every six months ($100 annually) for 30 years, and I will pay you back the initial $1,000 at the end of Year 30. By then, I will have paid you $3,000 ($100 × 30) plus your initial $1,000 for a total of $4,000. Since your profit is the $3,000 in interest (coupon) payments, you have made a profit of 300% after 30 years.

In other words, the longer you (the investor) have to go without the money that you lent to me (the government or company borrowing your money), then the higher the interest rate charged to me to compensate you for your trouble. This scenario plays out all the time with governments and companies all over the world. Raising large amounts of money and paying interest on the debt is how schools and highways get built and how many companies fund their operations.

If you'll notice, so far *bond* has been used to refer to T-Bills, T-Notes, and T-Bonds. This may seem confusing, but just remember that a bond is simply a debt instrument, even ones with different maturities and coupon payments. Whether it's issued by a government or a corporation, all bonds involve investors loaning money (by buying the bonds) and receiving payments of some kind for holding the bond.

Bond Prices and Interest Rates

So now that you understand the basics of how a bond works, let's look at bond prices. The price of a bond is determined by the general interest rate. For example, let's say you own a bond with a 30-year maturity that has an interest rate (coupon payment) of 4%. Since coupon payments are calculated based on the face value of a bond—usually $1,000—that means you will be paid $40 per year ($20 every six months) for 30 years for holding that bond because 4% of $1,000 is $40.

Now imagine that the Federal Reserve raises the general interest rate to 5%. That means that your bond's price will decrease because its interest rate is only 4%. Your bond's price decreases because when the general interest rate is raised to 5%, newly issued bonds will now have a 5% coupon payment. Your bond that only pays 4% isn't worth as much now because why would investors pay $1,000 for your 4% bond when they could spend the same $1,000 and get a 5% bond? Therefore, your bond's price—but not your coupon payment—will decrease. No matter how much interest rates go up in this example, you will still receive your $40 per year because your coupon payment is calculated using your bond's face value of $1,000 even though your bond's price is now lower than $1,000.

If you wanted to sell your 4% bond, you will end up receiving less than what you paid for it because the price has dropped. But keep in mind—and this is a very important concept—**bond yields and bond prices are inversely related**. That means that bond prices and bond yields move in opposite directions. When one goes up, the other goes down. When one goes down, the other goes up.

Note: If your bond's price falls below $1,000 because of rising interest rates, your bond is a **discount bond** because it trades for less than the normal face value of $1,000. And if your bond's price rises above $1,000 because of falling interest rates, then your bond is a **premium bond** because investors are willing to pay a premium of more than $1,000 to own it.

If interest rates increase to 5% and the price of your 4% bond goes down, this increases your bond's yield because yield is what you get when you divide the coupon payment by the price of the bond. So, if you're getting paid $40 per year with this bond but the bond's price drops to $900, then divide $40 by $900 to find the current yield. What do you get? 4.4%. Your yield has increased from 4% because your bond's price has gone down.

Why is this important? Because investors are always searching for high yields. If another investor wants to buy your bond that now has a 4.4% yield, it's a great deal for her because she's paying you $900 for the bond but still receiving $40 per year. Meanwhile, you had paid $1,000 for the bond to receive the same $40 per year.

But what happens when interest rates fall? Let's say that interest rates drop to 3%. Now your 4% bond will increase in price because it's more valuable. Other investors are willing to pay more for your bond than to pay for a newly issued bond with a 3% yield. But remember how bond prices and yields are inversely related? Say that your bond's price now increases from $1,000 to $1,100. That's great for you if you want to sell it to another investor, but your yield has decreased because the $40 annual coupon payment gives you a new yield of 3.6%, because $40/$1,100 = 3.6%. So, you are not getting as much "bang for your buck" in terms of yield. However, your 3.6% yield is still higher than the newly issued bonds with a 3% yield. Therefore, you will still attract investors if you want to sell your bond, and you'll make a $100 (or 10%) profit too.

And keep in mind that a smaller change in the interest rate (in either direction) will result in a smaller price change of the bond itself. A larger change in the interest rate (in either direction) will result in a larger price change of the bond itself. If the interest rate went up to 4.1% or down to 3.9%, the price of your 4% bond would only move a little. But if the interest rate went up to 5% or down to 3%, the price of your 4% bond would make a much bigger move.

What about the formulas to calculate how much your bond's price will change when interest rates change? Is it possible to predict how the price of a bond will change due to changes in interest rates? The answer is yes, but it's a complicated subject. I have included some relevant links in the back of the book when you feel comfortable researching that information. The important things to remember right now are the basics of how bonds work.

Yield to Maturity (YTM)

For bond investors, a key metric is a bond's **yield to maturity (YTM)**. The YTM of a bond is the calculated lifetime yield of a bond that assumes the investor receives all coupon payments and holds the bond until the maturity date.

Now, do you remember that the current yield of a bond was calculated by dividing the coupon payment by the current bond price? Well, the YTM is different from the current yield because the YTM factors in the present value of a bond. As you may recall, the present value indicates the current worth of a future stream of cash flows. By contrast, the current yield only tells you the rate of return at one point in time. So, the YTM is better because it will tell you the predicted overall rate of return for holding the bond until maturity. In other words, it's the lifetime yield.

As an example, assume you have a 20-year T-Bond. If its current yield is 3%, that just tells you that your coupon payment is 3% of the bond's current price. But if you discover that the YTM of the bond is 3.5%, you know that you will have a 3.5% return if you held the bond to maturity. So now you can compare your bond's YTM with the YTM of other bonds (or the rate of return on another kind of investment). If you found another bond of the same quality and maturity that had a YTM of 4%, then you may want to buy it after selling your 3.5% YTM bond. Remember, bond investors are generally on the lookout for higher yields, just as investors are constantly on the lookout for higher returns on their investments.

Let's look at an example for calculating YTM for a bond. Assume you're interested in a 20-year bond with an annual coupon rate of 5% that has a face value (par value) of $1,000 and that its current price is $700. Also assume it pays interest twice a year, as most bonds do. You can find specific YTM calculators for free like this one online: (**www.dqydj.com/bond-yield-to-maturity-calculator**). Enter the numbers in the proper blank spaces and hit Calculate. You should get a YTM of 8.04%. So if you bought this bond today and held it until maturity, that means it will have a ROI of 8.04% per year.

Treasury Inflation-Protected Securities (TIPS)

A popular group of Treasuries are what's known as Treasury Inflation-Protected Securities (TIPS). TIPS are designed to protect investors from inflation. As you may have learned at some point, inflation occurs when the prices of goods and services increase but purchasing power falls. Imagine you could previously buy bread at $4 a loaf, and then the price increases to $5 a loaf. Your wages haven't increased though, so that extra $1 is an inflationary cost to you. Inflation is bad because it makes you poorer even though you have the same amount of money, because the money you do have will not be able to buy as many things as it did before.

TIPS protect investors from inflation by increasing in price to match the rate of inflation. This is a very helpful feature for investors. Consider this: If you held a non-TIPS 30-year bond until maturity, you would receive $1,000 at the end of Year 30. But over 30 years, inflation would have increased dramatically, so that $1,000 wouldn't buy as much in 30 years as it would today. This is why TIPS are a great deal for bond investors. Keep in mind that if the price of your TIPS bond falls due to rising interest rates, then its price will still fall while also adjusting for inflation. Even though it accounts for inflation, it still otherwise operates by the same general rules as other bonds.

Zero-Coupon Bonds

So far, we've been talking about interest rates and coupon payments, but there's one type of bond that doesn't have either of those features: zero-coupon bonds. If you're not being compensated for lending money, what's the appeal of these particular bonds?

The answer is that zero-coupon bonds are deeply discounted. A zero-coupon bond does not pay interest or have coupon payments but instead pays its face value at maturity.

For example, a zero-coupon bond with a face value of $1,000 and a maturity of 10 years may be available for the highly discounted purchase price of $600, which is a discount of 40%. So, you would buy the bond for $600 and receive $1,000 (the face value) at the end of Year 10, with no coupon payments in between. The $600 you paid initially and the $1,000 you received at maturity (end of Year 10) means you made a profit of $400, because $1,000 − $600 = $400. The deep discount is the major advantage of this bond not having interest rates or regular coupon payments.

Here's another pop quiz for you. Given the choice of a zero-coupon bond with a maturity of 10 years versus a zero-coupon bond with a maturity of 20 years, which one will be cheaper to buy (have a bigger discount)? The answer is the one with a 20-year maturity. Since you won't be receiving coupon payments of any kind, asking you to go 20 years without them means the price will be discounted more than a zero-coupon bond with a 10-year maturity. For zero-coupon bonds, the longer the maturity, the bigger the discount.

Municipal Bonds (MUNIs)

It's not just the federal government that issues bonds to fund their operations. Whenever state and local governments need to borrow money to build schools or repair infrastructure, they issue municipal bonds (or MUNIs). Municipal bonds share the same basic features of Treasuries (coupon payments and maturities) but differ in a key way. Most municipal bonds are exempt from federal taxes as well as state and local taxes, provided you live in the state where the bond was issued. This tax-exempt status is a major advantage of most municipal bonds that investors love.

International Bonds

Just like the American government, foreign governments also issue bonds to cover the costs of their operations. There is a wide array of international bonds to choose from, with varying maturities, yields, and credit ratings, just like Treasuries. International bonds from developed economies (Canada, Australia, and most of Europe) are the safest, with lower yields because of their low odds of defaulting on their debt.

International bonds from emerging markets (India, China, Brazil, Russia, and others) offer higher yields due to their less-developed economies. But investors must also be wary of political and economic turmoil in many of these countries that can negatively affect their investment. Remember, higher yields generally mean higher risk.

Corporate Bonds

Finally, we come to corporate bonds. These are bonds issued by publicly traded companies to fund research and development, factory expansion, and other business activities. Just like Treasuries and municipal bonds, corporate bonds feature coupon payments and maturity dates. However, corporate bonds tend to be riskier. Because of this additional risk, they generally have higher yields than Treasuries and MUNIs with the same maturity dates.

That's because, unlike governments, corporations can go out of business. In the event of a bankruptcy, corporations may restructure in order to pay their debts. Bondholders are given priority in this case, though full repayment to bondholders is not always guaranteed. Unfortunately, stockholders are given last priority and generally lose their entire investment after a company's bankruptcy.

So now you understand the basics of how bonds work. Next, we'll look at two very popular investment vehicles: mutual funds and ETFs.

CHAPTER 6

MUTUAL FUNDS

You must be hungry by now, right? But you don't feel like cooking, so you have a choice on where to eat out: either the local steakhouse or the local buffet. If you go to the steakhouse, the steak you buy may turn out to be the greatest one you've ever had or it could be the worst. But if you go to the buffet, you'll have plenty of options to choose from. And if you place a dozen different buffet items on your plate, even if some of them aren't that good, you'll still be satisfied with your meal. The chances of you having a bad meal at a buffet are much lower than if you order one single steak at a restaurant.

In this example, eating the steak is like investing in a single stock. You're putting all your eggs in one basket (or all your steak on one plate). If the steak isn't good, then you've wasted your money. And hoping the steak will turn out well may be too risky considering all the money involved.

But at the buffet, you're given a large enough variety of food so that no one food item dominates, and the majority of good items will make up for the minority of bad ones. Your overall buffet experience wasn't ruined by any single item on its own. So, if eating at the steakhouse is like investing in a single stock, then eating at the buffet is like investing in a mutual fund.

A mutual fund is a type of investment vehicle that pools money from a large number of investors and invests it in a diversified portfolio on their behalf. Each investor owns a portion of the portfolio, depending on how much they have invested. The portfolio can include a mix of stocks, bonds, and other securities (or only stocks or only bonds, depending on the fund). Mutual funds are created with a specific investing objective in mind, like a "Mid-Cap Growth" fund or a "New Markets Income" fund. Fortunately, not only do mutual funds offer convenient diversification, but they are run by investment professionals from firms such as Vanguard and Fidelity. These professionals create the optimal fund that they believe will achieve the investment goals of their clients (actively managed funds) or offer a fund that replicates a stock index or bond index (passively managed funds or index funds).

Among the most popular types of mutual funds are those that reflect the stock market as a whole, such as the hypothetical Mutual Fund ABC below. This is an index fund, which is a type of mutual fund whose holdings reflect a specific index such as the S&P 500. This particular index fund is meant to reflect the entire domestic (American) equities market, and its holdings contain thousands of large, medium, and small stocks. This allows investors to have exposure to all these companies at once. As you can see in Figure 10, nearly all of Mutual Fund ABC's holdings are of US stocks.

Mutual Fund ABC

Asset Allocation

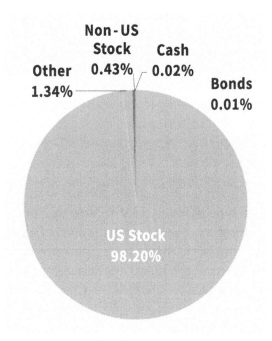

Figure 10

Let's look at some of Mutual Fund ABC's biggest holdings. As you can see in Figure 11, its top five holdings are: Company A, Company B, Company C, Company D and Company E. These five companies account for 9.96% of Mutual Fund ABC's total holdings. Do you see the word *weight*? That refers to what percentage of that particular stock accounts for the total holdings within the fund. Company A's stock, Mutual Fund ABC's biggest holding by weight, accounts for 2.5% of its total holdings. Each stock below it has a smaller weight, and since Mutual Fund ABC contains literally thousands of stocks, the weights for most of the stocks it holds would be less than 1% each. But when you add up all the holdings, the total is—you guessed it—100%.

And if you look at Figure 12, you'll see the weighted breakdown of Mutual Fund ABC by sector. It tells us that almost 75% of the fund is invested in stocks that are part of the technology, financial services, healthcare, consumer cyclical, and industrial sectors.

Mutual Fund ABC's top holdings

Company A weight	**2.50%**
Company B weight	**2.31%**
Company C weight	**1.98%**
Company D weight	**1.73%**
Company E weight	**1.44%**

Figure 11

Mutual Fund ABC's top sectors

Healthcare	**22.19%**
Financial Services	**17.13%**
Consumer Cyclical	**15.27 %**
Technology	**10.39%**
Industrials	**8.42%**

Figure 12

And since Mutual Fund ABC contains thousands of stocks, do you see how you are given broad exposure to the entire US stock market just by investing in this one mutual fund? Isn't that convenient? Because even if you had the money, imagine the time it would take to invest in these thousands of stocks individually. You would never leave the house, right? Furthermore, you would have to pay trading or transaction fees to buy all those stocks, which would reduce your profits substantially.

Now let's tackle some more mutual fund terms. While mutual funds are often a collection of stocks and/or bonds, there are some key differences between these two categories. First, how do you know how much one share in a mutual fund costs? To find out, we look at the mutual fund's net asset value (NAV).

Net Asset Value (NAV)

The NAV of a mutual fund is its price per share. It's calculated by taking the total assets within the fund, plus any cash that's in the fund, and subtracting the liabilities (any money the mutual fund has borrowed). The resulting number is then divided by the number of shares within the fund, which gives us the NAV.

Here's an example. Assume that the assets within a certain mutual fund total $90,000,000 and that they have cash totaling $20,000,000. They also have liabilities of $10,000,000 and a total of 5,000,000 shares. Using our formula: ($90,000,000 + $20,000,000 − $10,000,000 = $100,000,000; and $100,000,000/5,000,000 shares = $20). Therefore, the fund's NAV is $20. This is what you pay for one share of the fund.

Another key difference between mutual funds and stocks is when the price changes. The price of a stock can fluctuate throughout the trading day. But a mutual fund's NAV does not move at all during the trading day. When you see a mutual fund's NAV listed during trading hours, that is the NAV of the previous trading day. Now look at Figure 13, which lists information for Mutual Fund ABC after trading hours have ended. Do you see the NAV of $27.92? That's the NAV calculated after the close of today's trading session. And the previous close of $27.80 that's shown under the NAV was the NAV after yesterday's trading hours had ended.

Mutual Fund ABC
Net Asset Value (NAV): 27.92
+0.12 (+0.43%)

Previous Close	27.80
Open	27.83
Day Low/High	27.83/28.01
52-Week Low/High	24.32/28.15
YTD Return	20.29%
Net Assets	$2,341,958,421
1-Month Return	0.22%
1-Year Return	17.5%
Since Inception	9.04%

Figure 13

Now say you want to invest in Mutual Fund ABC. It certainly has things going for it. Check out its year-to-date (YTD) return of 20.29%. That's a phenomenal return by any measure. It's also outperforming its lifetime average return of 9.04% (indicated by Since Inception). It's also an index fund, which is among the least volatile kinds of mutual funds because it follows an entire market (like the S&P 500 index) instead of a niche market (like a technology fund would).

Imagine it's the following trading day and you're still interested in this mutual fund. But since the NAV hasn't been updated yet, you don't know what the price will be. But you can make an educated guess as to whether it will go up or down from $27.92. Since it's an index fund, check out some stocks mentioned in the fund's holdings. Better yet, check out the fund's top 10 holdings and then see how those particular stocks are doing during the trading day. If those stocks are going up, there's a good chance the fund's NAV will increase after the trading day ends. If they're going down, the NAV will probably decrease. Mutual funds typically update their NAVs between four p.m. and six p.m. Eastern (New York) time.

And remember, just because some of the stocks within a mutual fund go down in value, that does not mean that all of them do. Why? Because a mutual fund is diversified. The overall loss or gain in a mutual fund is somewhat limited because of the wide variety and number of stocks contained within it. Losses in one part of the fund can be offset by gains in the other part, and vice versa. Contrast that with buying a single stock, which could go on a wild ride in either direction in just one day.

Purchasing Mutual Fund Shares

If you want to purchase shares in a mutual fund, you need to make a bid to buy shares during the trading day or between trading sessions. Unlike with stocks, where you bid on the number of shares you want, bidding on a mutual fund involves entering a specific dollar amount you want to pay.

So, assuming you have a mutual fund account set up with a brokerage, imagine you want to invest $4,000 in a fund that has a NAV of $10 per share, so you would expect to get 400 shares. You bid $4,000 (before four p.m. Eastern time) and wait for the end of the trading day. Let's say the fund does well that day and the NAV increases to $10.50. Your $4,000 bid is then divided by $10.50 (the updated NAV) to give you 380.95 shares. Did you notice that's not quite 381 shares? That's because mutual funds, like stocks, can have fractional shares. In this case, you have 380 full mutual fund shares and 95% of another one. You've still spent the same $4,000 you would have, but you've received fewer shares than you originally expected because the NAV increased after the trading day ended. Likewise, if the NAV decreases the day you place your bid, you'll end up purchasing more than 400 shares.

What about withdrawing your money from a mutual fund? If you need to cash out part or all of your mutual fund shares, you submit a redemption request to the fund. Generally, the fund will give you back your money within seven business days. This is a longer process than when you sell stocks.

Not only are mutual funds diversified, but they also come in a wide variety of categories. They can focus only on stocks, only on bonds, or some combination of the two. They can also be classified by geography (so you can invest in securities from a specific country or region), value or growth objectives (safe dividend-paying securities or risky securities with higher returns), and size (small market cap stocks or large market cap ones), among other criteria. There are also many combinations of the above categories, and others too. No matter how specific your investment objective may be, there's a mutual fund for that.

Actively Managed Funds versus Passively Managed Funds

All mutual funds are managed by financial professionals. However, there is a key difference in how certain mutual funds are managed. There are two types of mutual funds when it comes to management styles: actively managed and passively managed.

An actively managed mutual fund is one in which professionals seek alpha, which are excess returns above the market. Remember how the S&P 500 represents the market as a whole? Well, pretend that the S&P 500 has an annual return of 2%, meaning an investor made a 2% profit that year if they invested in an S&P index fund. What a manager of an actively managed fund will do is create a fund comprised of various securities that they believe will have a higher return than the S&P 500.

These managers may claim that their actively managed fund will have a 3% annual return (which is an alpha of one because it's one percentage point higher than the market's 2% return). Their fund beating the market sounds great, doesn't it? Well, there's a catch. Actively managed mutual funds charge higher fees for their services. As an example, imagine an actively managed fund that promises a 2% return above and beyond the S&P 500, which last year produced a 2% return. You might think that you'd double your profits by investing in the actively managed fund, right?

Wrong. Although there are some actively managed funds that do very well, most tend to match or underperform the market. And what's worse, they charge you a flat fee regardless of how the fund performed. So, imagine that you invest $10,000 in this actively managed fund and it achieves a 4% return after one year, leaving you with $10,400 (because 4% of $10,000 is $400). And say the S&P 500 achieved a 2% return, just like it did last year, so the fund has a positive alpha of 2%, because 4% − 2% = 2%. Well, don't celebrate just yet. Because this hypothetical fund also charges you a 2% management fee that applies to your total assets within the fund. So the 2% fee is applied to the $10,400 you have after one year. 2% of $10,400 = $208. When you subtract that amount from $10,400, you get $10,192. So your final return is 1.92% because $192/$10,000 = 1.92%. And since investing in the S&P 500 would have netted you a 2% profit, the final 1.92% profit you made after the actively managed fund applied its fee leaves you worse off, even though the fund outperformed the S&P 500 index by 2%. And keep in mind that the fees from actively managed funds apply to your total assets within the fund. So the higher your profits in these funds, the more you'll pay in fees. And the more you pay in fees, the less money you will have to invest. In other words, you could have just invested in the S&P 500 directly and received a higher return. Furthermore, unless the fund managers consistently beat the market by more than 2% year after year after year, you'll continue to earn a lower ROI on your investment than you would earn by simply investing in an S&P 500 index fund.

So how would you do that? Simple. You invest in a passively managed index fund. A passively managed mutual fund is one that tracks an index such as the S&P 500. That's why they're commonly called index funds. It's called passive because it simply replicates the index's holdings. This is different from actively managed funds where the managers create a particular mix of securities that they think will beat the market. Since they want to beat the market, they are obviously not going to replicate the market the way a passively managed fund does.

Keep in mind that a passively managed fund still has fees. The difference is that their fees are much lower than those of an actively managed fund, typically around 0.5%. This is because a passive fund's managers are simply replicating the index instead of creating a specific portfolio like managers of active funds do.

And to prove how large fees can severely decrease the value of your investment, let's look at an example. Assume you invest $4,000 in a passively managed index fund that has a fee of 0.5%. Further assume that the fund has an average annual return (before the fee) of 5% and that you invest in the fund for 30 years. And let's say you invest an additional $1,000 at the beginning of every year.

Now go to the online financial calculator (**www.calculator.net/finance-calculator.html**) and enter 30 for N, $4,000 for Starting Principal, and $1,000 for PMT. Make sure to select "PMT made at the beginning of each compound period." Finally, enter 4.5% for I/Y (Interest). This is because you subtract the fund's 0.5% fee from the 5% return you make every year. Now click Calculate and you'll see that your Future Value after 30 years is $78,733.66. Impressive, isn't it?

But actively managed funds won't be so impressive. Pretend you invest the same $4,000 for the same 30 years while still investing $1,000 at the beginning of each year, just like the previous example. But this actively managed fund has an annual fee of 2%. Enter the same numbers as before in the financial calculator, except enter 3 for I/Y (Interest). This is because the fund's 2% annual fee is subtracted from the 5% annual return. Now click Calculate. You'll see that the actively managed fund will be worth $58,711.73 after 30 years. That's about $20,000 *less* than the passively managed fund. Despite the same amount of money and time involved in both funds, the fees in the actively managed fund have reduced your total return by roughly 25%.

Load versus No-Load Mutual Funds

Many mutual funds also have additional fees such as *load fees*. A *load fund* is one in which investors are either charged at the time of purchase (front-load) or at the moment they redeem, or sell, any shares in the fund (back-load). Load fees serve as a sort of sales commission for the fund's managers. There are also *no-load* funds, which do not have any kind of load fees.

If you don't want high fees to eat up your profits and you're fine with investing in the market itself, a no-load passively managed index fund would be the way to go. Warren Buffet has said many times that he recommends most investors simply invest in an index fund of US stocks because you'll get higher returns than you would with most actively managed mutual funds.

Now that you understand how mutual funds work, let's look at their financial "cousins" called exchange-traded funds, or ETFs.

CHAPTER 7

EXCHANGE-TRADED FUNDS (ETFs)

By now, you must think mutual funds are a great deal. They offer convenient diversification, and they come in a wide variety of categories. What's not to like?

There's a similar type of financial instrument that's skyrocketed in popularity in recent years: exchange-traded funds or ETFs. An ETF is very much like a mutual fund in many ways. All ETFs offer diversification by allowing you to own multiple stocks, bonds or both, and are available in numerous categories based on countries, sectors, and other factors. So why are they so popular?

A primary reason is because ETFs have lower fees than mutual funds. ETFs do not have any load fees whatsoever, unlike some mutual funds. And their operating expenses tend to be lower too. Another reason is because ETFs can be traded during the trading day because their prices fluctuate just like individual stocks. To put it another way, an ETF is basically a mutual fund that can be traded like a stock. It combines the best of both worlds to offer investors a convenient and affordable way to invest in the market.

Let's take a look at an example. Imagine you are risk-averse and want your portfolio to express that. A good option would be to invest in the bond market, which is not as risky as the stock market. One ETF that fits this bill is the hypothetical Bond ETF, whose asset allocation is shown on the left side of Figure 14.

Bond ETF Allocation by Sector

Bond Index Allocation by Sector

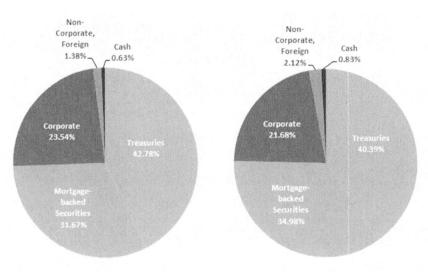

Figure 14

And on the right is a breakdown of the asset allocation of the underlying bond index itself. Both the ETF and the index have roughly the same weights for every category of fixed-income assets, whether they are Treasuries, mortgage-backed securities, or other investments. So, since the Bond ETF on the left has basically replicated the bond index on the right, what does that remind you of? A passively managed index fund. So that's a major way in which ETFs are similar to passively managed mutual funds. And as mentioned before, the diversification of ETFs is the other quality they share with mutual funds, whether those mutual funds are passively managed or actively managed.

But there are a few differences between ETFs and mutual funds, aside from the ones mentioned before. For one thing, the minimum investment required is much lower for ETFs. Since they are traded just like stocks, you can buy as little as one share at a time. Compare that with mutual funds, which require a minimum investment, usually several thousand dollars. So if you don't have that kind of money to invest but want to take advantage of diversification, then ETFs may be a better option for you.

Another difference is the possibility of saving money when purchasing ETFs. Since the NAV (price) of a mutual fund is calculated at the end of the trading day, you would end up paying the same price as everybody else. But with an ETF, you may be able to purchase it for a lower price during the trading day and watch it increase in value during the rest of the trading day. Of course, the ETF could also fall in value during the same period of time, so keep that in mind.

Generally speaking, ETFs are better for short-term investing and trading, while passively managed index funds are better for long-term investors who plan to buy and hold for many years.

CHAPTER 8

ORDER TYPES

If you are investing in single stocks or ETFs through an online brokerage like E*TRADE, there are different types of orders you can place when buying and/or selling: market orders, limit orders, stop orders, and trailing-stop orders.

Market Orders

A market order is one that is executed at the market price (the current price). For example, if you were interested in a stock that was trading at $15 per share, but you weren't too picky about paying a specific price for it, you would place a market order. Since stocks can make quick moves in either direction very quickly, you may end up paying more or less than $15 here with a market order. If the stock moved to $15.05 as soon as you placed your market order, you'd pay $15.05 per share instead of $15. But if it moved to $14.97, you'd pay that much instead of $15 per share.

Limit Orders

A limit order is one where the investor chooses a minimum or maximum price to execute their trade. For example, if a stock is trading at $20 per share, but you don't want to spend any more than $18 per share to buy it, then you would set a buy limit order for $18 per share. If the stock goes down to $18, your order will go through. But if it doesn't hit $18, your order will not go through. In other words, a buy limit order sets the maximum price per share that you are willing to pay.

What about selling at a certain price? That's where sell limit orders come in. A sell limit order involves setting the minimum price per share at which you are willing to sell a stock. Say that you own the stock in the previous example and had bought it when it was $15 per share. Now it's at $20 per share, and you're thinking of selling it for a profit. But you think it could go a little higher, so you decide to set a sell limit order for $21 per share. If the stock hits $21, your order will go through. If it doesn't hit $21, then you'll still own the shares.

Keep in mind that when it comes to either type of limit order, your limit price (the one you set) is just the threshold, meaning you could save even more money than you thought with a buy limit order or you could make a higher profit than you thought with a sell limit order.

Here's an example. Using the previous $20 stock, let's say you placed a buy limit order of $18 like before. At the end of the trading day, the stock has hit $18.02, only 2 cents away from your buy limit order, so it didn't go through. But imagine that at the beginning of the next trading day, the stock opens at $17.50. That means that not only does your buy limit order go through, but you saved 50 cents per share because it's 50 cents lower than your $18 buy limit order. So you saved some extra money in this scenario.

If you placed a sell limit order of $21, imagine that the stock hits $20.92 cents at the end of the trading day. Your order doesn't go through, but what if the stock opened the next day at $22 per share? Your sell limit order would go through, and you'd make $1 more per share than you would have otherwise. So you made more money in this scenario.

Stop Orders

What if you want your order to go through at a very specific price, one that's not above or below it, but exactly at that amount? That's where stop orders come in. A stop order is one where you select a specific price at which you want to buy or sell your stock. Here's an example.

If you own 100 shares of the previously mentioned stock that's trading at $20, perhaps you're worried that the price will fall soon. Say you place a stop order for $19. This means that if the stock drops to $19, your shares will automatically be sold at that price. So you would only lose $1 per share that you own for a total loss of $100. If you hadn't placed the stop order and the stock nosedived to $15 per share, you'd lose $5 per share. And if you sold at that point, you'd have lost $500. A sell stop order is a great way to limit potential losses, particularly if you don't have time to constantly check stock prices.

You can also place a buy stop order. This involves setting a specific price that you want to buy the stock at. The difference between a buy stop order and a buy limit order is that the limit order involves the maximum price you would be willing to pay per share, which is usually lower than the current price per share. By contrast, a buy stop order involves you setting a price above the current stock price that you're willing to pay.

So why would you place a buy stop order and pay a higher price instead of buying the stock now when it's cheaper? A major reason is that traders are waiting to see if the stock can break through a certain price point. So if the stock is trading at $20 and you set your buy stop order to $22, that means you think the stock's momentum will carry it past $22 per share once it hits that amount. Fans of technical analysis often use these types of buy stop orders when trading stocks or other investments.

Trailing Stop Orders

A similar type of stop order is the trailing stop order. A trailing stop order is similar to a stop order except for one key feature. Instead of setting a specific price to buy or sell at, a trailing stop order sets a specific percentage or dollar amount to determine when to enter or exit a trade, and this sell order also trails the stock's price by that specified amount. Here's an example.

Say you own 100 shares of the previous stock that's trading at $20 per share. You're worried that the price may drop and you'll lose money, but you also don't want to sell too early and miss out on any profits if the stock rebounds. So what do you do? You enter a trailing stop sell order. Imagine that you are willing to lose $200 at most with this stock. Since you own 100 shares, a $200 loss involves the price dropping by $2 per share ($2 × 100 shares = $200).

So you enter a trailing stop sell order of $2 per share. If the stock dropped by $2 to $18 per share, your shares would automatically be sold. But what happens if the stock moves to $21 per share? This is the magic of the trailing stop. Since the latest and highest price since placing your order is $21 per share and your trailing stop is for $2, then the lowest price your shares would automatically sell at is $19 per share. Do you see why? Your $2 trailing stop means your stock will be sold if it's $2 below the highest price reached since you placed the trailing-stop order. Since $21 − $2 = $19, that's the price your shares would be sold at.

Let's say the stock then drops to $20.50. Your shares would still be sold if it hits $19 because it's $2 behind the highest price of $21 per share. But if the stock then jumps to $21.75, your shares would be sold if the stock fell back down to $19.75, because $21.75 − $2 = $19.75. The trailing stop is constantly trailing the most recent highest achieved price, hence the name.

A buy trailing stop order works in the opposite direction. However, like a buy stop order, this type of order is rarely used and is best for more sophisticated investors, so we won't cover it here.

Day and Good-Til-Canceled Orders

One final note about placing orders. Every online brokerage firm allows you one of two options when choosing an order type: day and good til canceled (GTC). So if you set a specific order type (limit, trailing stop, etc.) but only wanted it to go through that day (if it goes through at all), you'd choose day. But if you want your order type to be in effect until you manually cancel it, then choose GTC.

CHAPTER 9

INVESTMENT TAXES

All the information in this book must make you look forward to making and investing money, right? Now you just need to make sure you learn how to keep the money you earn from your investments. That means dealing with one of the inevitable things in life—taxes.

In most investments, you are required to pay taxes on your profits, also known as capital gains. There are two broad categories of capital gains taxes: short-term and long-term, depending on how soon you sell your stocks, bonds, mutual funds, or ETFs.

Short-Term Capital Gains Taxes

Short-term capital gains refer to profits on securities sold less than one year after you bought them. Your tax rate on these profits would depend on your highest federal income tax bracket. The 2019 federal income tax brackets in the United States are shown in Figure 15.

Rate	Single Individual	Married Filing Jointly	Married Filling Separately	Head of Household Filing
10%	$0–$9,700	$0–$19,400	$0–$9,700	$0–$13,850
12%	$9,700–$39,475	$19,400–$78,950	$9,700–$39,475	$13,850–$52,850
22%	$39,475–$84,200	$78,950–$168,400	$39,475–$84,200	$52,850–$84,200
24%	$84,200–$160,725	$168,400–$321,450	$84,200–$160,725	$84,200–$160,700
32%	$160,725–$204,100	$321,450–$408,200	$160,725–$204,100	$160,700–$204,100
35%	$204,100–$510,300	$408,200–$612,350	$204,100–$306,175	$204,100–$510,300
37%	$510,300 and over	$612,350 and over	$306,175 and over	$510,300 and over

Figure 15

To find your highest tax bracket, first determine whether you're filing as a single person, jointly filing with your spouse, or filing as head of household. Then find your income within the ranges given in each column.

Let's look at an example. Imagine you are single and making $50,000 a year at your job. That puts you in the 22% tax bracket because your $50,000 income is between $39,475 and $84,200, so that is your highest tax bracket. Now pretend that you bought $2,000 worth of stock six months ago. In those six months, your $2,000 investment has grown to $2,500 for a profit of $500, right? If you were to sell your $2,500 worth of stock now, just six months after you bought it, your short-term capital gains are your $500 profit. And since you are in the 22% tax bracket, your short-term capital gains taxes owed would be $110. That's because $500 × 22% = $110.

Long-Term Capital Gains Taxes

But what if you held on to that stock for more than a year? Not only would your investment be likely to grow further, but you would also owe less in taxes if you sell at any point beyond one year. That's because long-term capital gains—referring to profits on securities sold at least one year after you bought them—feature lower tax rates. Look at Figure 16. These are the long-term capital gains tax rates for 2019.

Rate	Single Individual	Married Filing Jointly	Head of Household
0%	$0–$39,375	$0–$78,750	$0–$52,750
15%	$39,375–$434,550	$78,750–$488,850	$52,750–$461,700
20%	$434,550 and over	$488,850 and over	$461,700 and over

Figure 16

Do you see that there are only three different tax rates here? And that many people fall into the 0% bracket for long-term capital gains if their regular income is low enough? And based on this table, most people would pay a 15% long-term capital gains rate in the worst case? You'd have to be earning over $434,550 per year in income (which very few people do) to pay the highest long-term capital gains rate of 20%. It's generally in your best interest to hold off on selling your investments for at least one year to save money on capital gains taxes.

Assume you bought $5,000 worth of stock and sold it more than a year later for $7,000. Further assume that you are filing as Head of Household and your income is $100,000. According to Figure 16, your long-term capital gains tax rate is 15%. Since you made a $2,000 profit, you would owe $300 in capital gains taxes. This is because $2,000 × 15% = $300.

But if you had instead sold the stock less than a year after you bought it, your short-term rate would have been 24%, meaning you'd owe $480 ($2,000 × 24%). Do you see the advantage of long-term capital gains rates versus short-term ones?

Note: United States taxpayers in the highest bracket may also be subject to a 3.8% additional tax rate on long-term investments. This is a feature of the Affordable Care Act, better known as "Obamacare." Not all people in this group are subject to this extra tax, but some are, depending on the amount of their adjusted gross income and net investment income.

Long-term capital gains rates provide a better deal for the investor from a tax perspective. Obviously, certain emergencies may require you to liquidate your stocks within a year, but as long as you are not losing money on your investments, it's more advantageous to hold off on selling them for at least a year.

Tax Deductions for Investment Losses

Now you might be thinking, "What if I lose money on my investments?" How do taxes work in that case? Well, the good news is that you wouldn't owe a capital-gains tax because you didn't have any capital gains. Furthermore, you can apply your losses as a tax deduction for up to $3,000 per year.

So, if you had exactly $3,000 in investment losses for the year, you can use the entire loss to reduce your taxable income by $3,000. But if you had, say, $8,000 in investment losses that year, you'd only be able to reduce your taxable income by $3,000 per tax year. You can "carry over" any additional losses in future tax years, so if you lost $6,000 on your portfolio this year, you could deduct $3,000 in taxes this year and next year. If you had $1,000 in losses, you could reduce your taxable income by $1,000 this tax year.

Dividends and Capital Gains Taxes

Don't forget that if you own any dividend-paying stocks, you will owe short-term capital gains taxes when you receive ordinary dividends. That's because you are receiving dividends every quarter (every three months), which is less than a year. Again, your rates are contingent on your highest federal tax rate.

However, you will pay long-term capital gains rates on qualified dividends. A qualified dividend is one that meets certain criteria, one of which is the investor holding the dividend-paying stock for at least 60 days and starting 60 days before the most recent ex-dividend date. If you'll recall, the ex-dividend date is the date on which investors cannot receive dividends for the most recent quarter if they buy the stock on or after this date. But instead of breaking out the calendar, just remember that most dividend-paying stocks already offer qualified dividends. So, you can enjoy the benefits of long-term capital gains rates while owning many dividend-paying stocks.

CHAPTER 10

RETIREMENT AND SAVINGS PLANS

Investing is best used as a long-term strategy to build wealth and financial freedom. Whether you're investing for your retirement that's decades away or saving up for your child's college education, patience is the key because compound interest becomes exponentially more rewarding over time. There are popular investing vehicles out there that allow you to invest for the long term. We'll examine a few of them, and you might be surprised at their benefits.

Traditional 401(k)

What if I told you that you have a good chance of receiving free money for years and years? And what if I told you that this free money came from your employer? Sounds too good to be true, right? But not only is it true, it's extremely common in America and is known as a 401(k). **A 401(k) is an employer-offered retirement plan that workers can periodically invest in while their employer matches their contributions.**

Here's how it works. Imagine you work at Company XYZ. Your boss tells you that you can contribute a portion of your earnings every paycheck to your 401(k) and the company will match your contribution up to 3% of your pretax earnings.

You look at Company XYZ's 401(k) information and see that they offer various mutual funds with different asset classes and investment objectives. After choosing a mutual fund or funds, you tell your boss that you will contribute 3% of your pretax earnings every paycheck through a Traditional 401(k). So if your gross salary (your salary before taxes) is $1,000 per paycheck, then

$30 ($1,000 × 3%) will be taken out of your paycheck and invested into the 401(k) every time you receive your paycheck.

Your $30 contribution means your taxable income (your income subject to taxes) would now be $970 ($1,000 − $30). Do you see the benefit here? You contribute a small amount to your retirement every paycheck, and in exchange you will end up paying less in income taxes. But it gets even better.

Since your company matches your 401(k) up to 3%, then that means your company will also contribute $30 to your 401(k) every time you do. And the only thing you have to do to keep receiving their matching contribution is to stay with the company. So that's free money that your company is offering you. Do you remember how increasing your principal on a regular basis will allow compound interest to maximize your profits? This is the same idea, because not only are you adding to your principal every two weeks, but so is your company.

Of course, you can contribute more than 3% if you want. But keep in mind that companies that offer 401(k)s limit their contributions. So, in the previous example, if you contributed 5% per paycheck, you would invest $50 every two weeks, but your company would only invest $30 (3%) each time. Still, that's free money that your company is giving you. And while many companies, large and small, offer 401(k)s, there are a shocking amount of people who choose not to invest in them. So, they're basically throwing free money away.

Remember, the time value of money is more effective the sooner you invest. So a 25-year-old investing in a 401(k) and receiving matching employer contributions will end up with far more money by retirement than someone who starts at the age of 45. And don't think that having a 401(k) means you have to stay with your company forever. You can roll over your 401(k) when you move to a new company as long as they also offer a 401(k) plan.

The maximum you can contribute to your 401(k) per year is $18,000. But that limit does not include your employer's total matching contribution for that year.

Roth 401(k)

I mentioned earlier that traditional 401(k) contributions are pretax. The advantage is that you contribute your pretax earnings (and lower your taxable income each paycheck) and only pay taxes on your 401(k) when you withdraw money from it at retirement. But what if you don't want to pay huge taxes when you retire? There's a solution to that. It's called a Roth 401(k). **A Roth 401(k) is one in which your contributions are made with post-tax earnings and where you don't pay taxes at retirement when you withdraw your money.**

Using the same example as before, let's look at your gross paycheck of $1,000. Pretend that your total tax rate is 20%, and so you end up with $800 after taxes (because 20% of $1,000 = $200 and $1,000 − $200 = $800). So if you agreed to invest 3% in a Roth 401(k), then you would contribute $24 ($800 × 3%) per paycheck. So only after all taxes were taken out did you contribute your 3%, right? And while that $24 may be less than the $30 you contributed to the Traditional 401(k), you won't have to pay any taxes at retirement because you were already taxed when contributing to your Roth 401(k).

A Roth 401(k) is very advantageous for younger employees. That's because when you're young, you are likely to be making very little money and therefore your tax rate is already low. Therefore, contributing your post-tax earnings is not a huge burden because of the insignificant amount of taxes you pay at that point. And since a traditional 401(k) would tax you at retirement based on your most recent income (which would be much bigger than your income when you were in your 20s), a Roth 401(k) means you can avoid that massive tax bill when you start to withdraw your money during retirement. Keep in mind, though, if your employer matches any part of your contribution to a Roth 401(k), their contributions will be taxed at retirement, unlike your contributions.

Traditional IRAs and Roth IRAs

Now let's look at similar investment vehicles: IRAs. An IRA (or individual retirement account) is like a 401(k) in that you can contribute your pretax earnings toward it and pay taxes at retirement.

A Roth IRA is similar to a Roth 401(k) in that you contribute your post-tax earnings towards it and don't pay taxes upon retirement. Both traditional and Roth IRAs also offer investing opportunities in mutual funds and other investment vehicles just like 401(k)s do.

However, there are some key differences between an IRA and a 401(k). First, unlike a 401(k), employers cannot match your contribution to a traditional IRA. Second, the annual contribution limit to a traditional IRA or Roth IRA is $5,500 (or $6,500 if you are over the age of 50). This is in contrast to a traditional or Roth 401(k) where the annual contribution limit (excluding employer matching) is $18,000.

So it's obvious that both types of IRAs don't go very far compared to either type of 401(k). But that doesn't mean you shouldn't take advantage of IRAs. If your financial situation allows it, you should contribute to your employer's 401(k) and an IRA that will act as a supplemental retirement plan. Remember, every dollar you invest now will be worth much more decades from now. And, because of the tax benefits that come from investing in IRAs and 401(k)s, your money will compound and grow much more over time.

529 Plans (College Savings Plans)

For many parents out there, saving for their children's college education can seem like a monumental task. Aside from the skyrocketing tuition that will only climb higher in the future, it can be difficult to understand how to save properly for this major event in their children's lives.

Fortunately, every state in America has what's known as a 529 Plan. A 529 Plan is an investment plan that you can contribute to just like an IRA or 401(k), but for the sole purpose of paying for your child's college education or your own.

These plans have similarities with IRAs and 401(k)s, along with some differences. Some of the similarities include the ability to invest in mutual funds. You can allocate your funds however you see fit.

But the key differences are striking. In a 529 Plan, you will not be taxed on the federal level when you withdraw the money to pay for your or your child's education. After all, that would be less money for college, which isn't getting any cheaper. You may be taxed at the state level upon withdrawal, though dozens of states currently allow you to take the money as a deduction or tax credit.

Though it varies state by state, there is no single clearly defined annual contribution limit in a 529 Plan. Remember the $18,000 annual limit for a 401(k) or the $5,500 annual limit for an IRA? There's no specific limit in a 529 Plan, at least in the federal sense. However, 529s do have lifetime limits, and all expenses must be used solely for college tuition and/or college-related expenses such as books and housing. And keep in mind, a 529 Plan does not require you to have a college-bound child. If you envision going to college yourself as an older adult, you can invest in a 529 Plan because there are no age limits.

But what if you have excess funds left over in your 529 plan after you've paid for your child's college tuition? You can use that money for the education of your other children or even your grandchildren further down the line. But if you wanted to withdraw your excess funds for reasons other than college, your withdrawals are subject to a 10% penalty.

So, whether you need to pay for your child's education or just your own, a 529 Plan is an effective way to do so.

CHAPTER 11

INVESTING STRATEGIES

So now that we've covered the basics of investing, why don't we put them into action? If you've decided to enroll in a 401(k) through your employer, all you have to do is fill out the paperwork, and they'll take care of the rest. But if you'd like to invest on your own, you can create an account with one of many online brokerages out there.

But before investing in a 401(k) or going through an online brokerage, you'll need to determine your investing strategy. Are you a conservative investor (meaning you don't like risk)? Are you an aggressive investor (meaning you don't mind risk)? Or are you a moderate investor, somewhere in between? Here are some basic strategies for each type of investor. Keep in mind that these are just general suggestions that fit the investor profiles and do not have to be followed to the exact letter.

Conservative Investing Strategies

First let's look at a conservative investing strategy. Since conservative investors don't like risk, they don't want to invest in risky securities. So how should they allocate their portfolio?

As you may remember, bonds are considered safer, or less risky, than stocks. So, a conservative investor may want to invest anywhere from 35% to 50% of their portfolio within bonds, whether it be in individual bonds, bond mutual funds, or bond ETFs. Also, investing in Treasuries (US government bonds) would be preferable versus corporate bonds or emerging market bonds, which are much riskier. Money market accounts (containing short-term bonds) should also be utilized to take advantage of their extreme levels of safety. And conservative investors will also benefit from the regular bond coupon payments as a steady source of income.

As far as stocks go, conservative investors should invest roughly 20% to 35% of their portfolio in them. The more conservative an investor is, the more they should consider mutual funds or ETFs because of their diversification. A passively managed index fund or ETF that replicates the S&P 500 would be a good bet. If these investors would still like to invest in individual stocks, they should choose stable dividend-paying value stocks that have a beta of less than 1.

Even conservative investors should have some exposure to the international market through 5% to 15% of their portfolio. Since they don't want to risk too much, investing in foreign government bonds from developed countries would be a good start. They offer low yields but high stability. There are many mutual funds and ETFs for this purpose.

Finally, all investors (even aggressive ones) should have cash as part of their trading strategy. Always be sure to keep some cash on hand in your portfolio so that you have money if you need it, and so you can take advantage of great buying opportunities if there's a big market crash or recession. For a conservative investor, keeping 10% to 20% of their portfolio in cash would be wise. This cash can earn interest in a brokerage account. And in case of emergencies, it's much easier to withdraw this money versus withdrawing money after selling stocks, bonds, mutual funds, or ETFs.

Moderate Investing Strategies

Now let's look at a moderate investing strategy, one in which you want to risk more than a conservative investor but not nearly as much as an aggressive investor.

The moderate investor should invest 20% to 35% of their funds in bonds. This will provide somewhat of a counterweight to any volatile movement when it comes to stocks in their portfolio. And since they are more accepting of risk, they should seek a 50/50 split between Treasuries and corporate bonds. The corporate bonds will provide higher yields while the Treasuries will provide greater stability. Moderate investors may also want to allocate a small portion of their bond portfolio to emerging-market bonds so they can experience a bit more risk.

As for stocks, moderate investors should invest 45% to 60% of their funds in this category. Passively managed index funds should be a part of the portfolio, though these investors can also invest a greater portion in single stocks compared to conservative investors.

Specifically, moderate investors should evenly split their single-stock allocation between value stocks and growth stocks, those which are known for higher returns and an equivalent amount of risk. That's because growth stocks are—compared to value stocks—overvalued when comparing their prices versus their fundamental valuation.

Remember the PE ratio? Growth stocks will have a higher PE ratio than value stocks. People are willing to pay far more for growth stocks than what they are worth on paper because growth stocks are more likely to increase in price over time thanks to the nature of accelerating compound growth. Value stocks, on the other hand, are more stable in price and appeal to investors because of their low volatility and consistent dividends.

When it comes to international stocks, moderate investors should allocate 20% to 30% of their funds. A larger exposure to the international market—even those of developed countries—adds some risk to the portfolio.

Finally, the moderate investor should invest 10% to 15% in cash. This is enough of a cushion for this particular investing strategy.

Aggressive Investing Strategies

When it comes to the aggressive investor, he or she wants to take high risks to—possibly—achieve high rewards. In other words, the aggressive investing approach is like walking on a tightrope toward an enormous bag of money waiting on the other side. Just be sure you don't fall, okay?

Since bonds present the least amount of risk, aggressive investors should only invest 10% to 20% of their funds in this category. This presents a much smaller safety cushion versus conservative and moderate strategies, but the goal of an aggressive investor is capital appreciation, that is, growing their money. The greater the risk is, the higher the reward (or the bigger the loss) in most investments. Emerging-market bonds may be an attractive option for these investors because of their high-risk/high-yield qualities.

Aggressive investors should allocate 60% to 75% of their portfolio to stocks. With this investing strategy, mutual funds and ETFs may be ignored in favor of single stocks. The more that this investor puts his money in single stocks, the riskier the strategy. Growth stocks would obviously constitute most or all of this portion of the portfolio because they are known for high capital appreciation when they actually perform well. And since growth stocks tend to have betas higher than 1, a successful growth investor may find it easier to achieve alpha and beat the market.

Emerging-market stocks also favor aggressive investors. They can be included within the 60% to 75% allocated to stocks in your portfolio. The easiest way to purchase them would be through a relevant mutual fund or ETF. But remember that this diversification does not reduce risk to the extent that mutual funds or ETFs normally do. In good economic times, emerging-market securities tend to perform well. But in bad economic times—or even in reaction to one-time news events—investors will flock to safer investments. That means emerging-market securities are the first to fall after a crisis because they are less safe than securities from developed countries.

Finally, the aggressive investor should set aside 5% to 10% of their portfolio as cash. Essentially, the more aggressive the strategy, the less money allocated to cash, as well as bonds and other safer instruments.

CHAPTER 12

CONCLUSION

I hope you've learned a lot from this book. In the modern age, financial literacy is more vital than ever to living a successful life. With the knowledge you've acquired from this book, you should be able to understand the building blocks of investing and the freedom it can bestow upon you.

Remembering and using the basic terms and concepts we've covered here will help you secure your financial future. My goal in writing this book was to demystify the world of investing and make it accessible to anyone and everyone.

We all started at 0 in life, and it's up to us to save and invest our money so we can achieve financial freedom and independence in life. Where you choose to go from here is up to you. It's my greatest wish that *One Hour Investor* has helped you take the first step in one of the most important journeys of your life.

I wish you the best of luck in all your investing endeavors. Thank you for allowing me to bring this message to you.

INVESTING RESOURCES AND ADDITIONAL INFORMATION

FINANCIAL CALCULATORS

General Financial Calculator: **www.calculator.net/finance-calculator.html**

Yield to Maturity (YTM) Calculator: **www.dqydj.com/bond-yield-to-maturity-calculator**

WEBSITES

These are some of the best investing websites out there you can use to research stocks and further your financial education.

The Motley Fool: **www.fool.com**

Investopedia: **www.investopedia.com**

Morningstar: **www.morningstar.com**

Seeking Alpha: **www.seekingalpha.com**

ONLINE BROKERAGES

E*TRADE: **www.etrade.com**

TD Ameritrade: **www.tdameritrade.com**

Fidelity: **www.fidelity.com**

Charles Schwab: **www.schwab.com**

BOOKS

The Intelligent Investor by Benjamin Graham

The Bond Book by Annette Thau

A Random Walk Down Wall Street by Burton G. Malkiel

The Little Book of Common Sense Investing by John C. Bogle

The Smartest 401(k) Book You'll Ever Read by Daniel R. Solin

How Technical Analysis Works by Bruce M. Kamich

EDUCATIONAL VIDEOS

How the Economic Machine Works by Ray Dalio:
www.youtube.com/watch?v=PHe0bXAIuk0

How to Read a Financial Statement:
www.youtube.com/watch?v=Jkse-Wafe9U

How Technical Analysis Works:
www.youtube.com/watch?v=rlZRtQkfK04

GLOSSARY

BASIC FINANCIAL CONCEPTS

Compound Interest: Interest that is applied to both the principal and previously earned interest.

Compounding: Taking a known present value, ROI, and time period to find an unknown future value (i.e., finding how much you'll have in the future based on what you invest today).

Discounting: Taking a known future value, ROI, and time period to find an unknown present value (i.e., finding how much you need to invest today to get a specific amount in the future).

Future Value (FV): The amount earned (or desired) at a future date after compounding.

Payment Value (PMT): The amount paid on a consistent basis in a financial calculation, such as regular deposits.

Present Value (PV): The current value of a future stream of cash flows. Present value is always smaller than the future value because of the time value of money.

Principal: The initial (and/or ongoing) amount invested in a security or account.

Return on Investment (ROI): The profit earned on an investment, expressed as a percentage (marked as INT on financial calculators).

Rule of 72: This rule determines how long an investment takes to double. You can calculate how long it takes for an investment to double by dividing 72 by the ROI.

Time Value of Money (TVM): The concept that a dollar today is worth more than a dollar tomorrow (i.e., the sooner you invest, the better).

BASIC FINANCIAL STATEMENTS

Asset: Something owned by a company that's used to generate profits.

Balance Sheet: Lists a company's assets, liabilities, and owner's equity at a given point in time.

Expenses: Money paid to keep the company running, such as rent, wages, and equipment.

Income Statement: Lists revenues and expenses to find net income; issued quarterly.

Liability: Something owed by a company to others, such as employees' wages and business loans.

Net Income (Net Profit or Earnings): The result of revenue minus all expenses; the "bottom line" profit.

Owner's Equity: With publicly traded companies, the portion of a company's assets that has been paid for by shareholders (stockholders).

Revenue: Money received by a company through their normal operations.

Statement of Cash Flows (CFS): Indicates cash flowing in and out of a company from operations, investing and financing.

STOCKS

1-Year Target Estimate: The estimate set by finance professionals of a stock's price in one year.

52-Week Range: The range that a stock's price moved within the course of one year.

Average Volume: The average number of shares that are normally traded.

Beta: The volatility of a stock versus the market; beta < 1 is less volatile, beta > 1 is more volatile.

Blue Chip Company: A long-existing company with stable reputation and financial performance.

Day's Range: The range that a stock's price moved within the trading day.

Dividend: Quarterly amount per share paid to investors; set in advance.

Dividend Reinvestment Program (DRIP): Reinvests investor dividends to buy more shares.

Earnings per Share (EPS): The amount per share allocated to earnings.

Ex-Dividend Date: The date from which no dividends paid in next quarter if stock is not owned.

Market (S&P 500): The 500 largest publicly traded companies that represent the market as a whole.

Market Capitalization: The size of a publicly traded company; the number of shares times price per share.

Open: The price at which a stock opens at the beginning of a new trading day.

Outstanding Number of Shares: The shares of stock available to investors and company founders.

Previous Close: The price at which a stock closed at on the previous trading day (Monday through Friday).

Price-Earnings Ratio (PE ratio): The price per share divided by earnings per share; the multiple that investors are willing to pay per $1 of earnings.

Privately Owned Company: A company owned by one person or a small group of people.

Publicly Traded Company: A company that sells shares of stock to investors.

Stock: Partial ownership in a publicly traded company.

Volume: The number of shares traded (bought and sold) within one trading day.

Yield (Dividend): Dividend per share divided by price per share; the higher the yield, the more attractive to investors.

BONDS

Bond: A debt instrument purchased by an investor (lender) who receives regular interest payments in return for loaning the money.

Bond Price: The price of a bond; can change based on the prevailing interest rates.

Bond Rating: A rating assigned to a specific bond based on creditworthiness of the issuer (borrower).

Corporate Bonds: Bonds issued by corporations to fund business activities.

Coupon (Interest) Payment: A regular payment made to most bond investors for holding the bond.

Discount Bond: A bond that sells below $1,000 because its coupon is less than the prevailing interest rate.

Emerging-Market Bonds: Bonds from developing economies; subject to volatility and instability.

Face Value: The price of a bond (typically $1,000) that is paid on the maturity date to the investor, in addition to all previous coupon payments paid to the investor.

Inflation: A rise in the cost of goods and services.

Interest Rate (Bond): The borrowing rate that determines the size of coupon payments for bondholders; the higher the interest rate, the higher the payment (in absolute dollars).

International Bonds: Bonds issued by foreign companies or governments.

Maturity Date: The specific date that a bond's principal is paid back at face value to whomever owns the bond.

Maturity Ladder: A series of bonds with differing maturity dates.

Municipal Bonds (MUNIs): Bonds issued by state or city governments; usually tax-exempt.

Premium Bond: A bond that sells above $1,000 because its coupon is more than the prevailing interest rate.

Ratings Agencies: Agencies such as Moody's that rate bonds to inform investors of the bond issuers' creditworthiness.

T-Bills (Treasury Bills): US government-issued bonds with maturities of less than one year.

T-Bonds (Treasury Bonds): US government-issued bonds with maturities between 10 and 30 years.

T-Notes (Treasury Notes): US government-issued bonds with maturities between 1 and 10 years.

Treasuries: Various bonds issued by the United States government to fund their operations.

Treasury Inflation-Protected Securities (TIPS): Treasuries that also adjust in price to match inflation.

Yield (Bond): A bond's coupon payment divided by the bond's current price; the lower the bond price, the higher the yield (and more attractive to investors).

Yield to Maturity (YTM): The lifetime yield of a bond if held to maturity and all coupon payments are made.

Zero-Coupon Bonds: Deeply discounted bonds; no coupon payments; face value is paid at maturity.

MUTUAL FUNDS

Actively Managed Fund: A fund created and managed by professionals who seek alpha; high fees can be involved.

Alpha: A return on investment (ROI) above the return of the S&P 500 (market as a whole).

Growth Fund: A mutual fund specializing in riskier securities known for generating high returns.

Load Fund: A fund that charges upfront fees (front-load) or when shares sold by investor (back-load).

Mutual Funds: Professionally managed and diversified fund owned by its many investors; its diversification makes it much more stable than a single stock.

Net Asset Value (NAV): The price per share of a mutual fund; calculated after the trading day ends.

No-Load Fund: A fund that does not charge load fees of any kind.

Passively Managed Fund (Index Fund): It replicates a stock index or bond index; low fees are involved.

Redemption Request: An investor's request to sell his or her shares in a mutual fund.

Value Fund: A mutual fund specializing in low-growth but stable stocks that often pay dividends.

ETFs

ETF (Exchange-traded Fund): A diversified mutual fund that can be traded like a stock.

Sector: A specific industry, such as technology, that many ETFs and mutual funds are based on.

FUNDAMENTAL ANALYSIS VERSUS TECHNICAL ANALYSIS

Death Cross: A bearish (negative) signal when the 50-day MA crosses below the 200-day MA.

Fundamental Analysis: It examines a company's financial statements, competitors, and the economy.

Golden Cross: A bullish (positive) signal when the 50-day MA crosses above the 200-day MA.

Moving Average (MA): The updating price average of a timeframe (10-day, 50-day, 200-day, etc.).

Technical Analysis: It examines technical indicators like price, volume, and moving averages.

RETIREMENT AND SAVINGS PLANS

529 Plan: An investment/savings plan whose contributions pay for college costs.

Roth 401(k): An investment plan funded by post-tax contributions and matched by employer; investors are not taxed at retirement (except for employer contributions).

Roth IRA: An individual retirement plan funded by post-tax contributions.

Traditional 401(k): An investment plan funded by pre-tax contributions and matched by employer; investors are taxed at retirement.

Traditional IRA: An individual retirement account funded with pretax contributions.

INVESTMENT TAXES

Dividend Taxes: Short-term capital gains taxes paid on some quarterly dividends.

Long-Term Capital Gains Taxes: Taxes paid on investments sold more than a year after purchase; lower than short-term rates.

Qualified Dividend Taxes: Long-term capital gains taxes paid on qualified dividends.

Short-Term Capital Gains Taxes: Taxes paid on investments sold less than a year after purchase; higher than long-term rates.

Tax Deduction (for Investment Losses): A limit of $3,000 in investing losses that can reduce taxable income.

ORDER TYPES

Day order: An order that indicates any of the below orders should only take place (if achieved) on that day.

Good-til-Canceled (GTC) order: An order that indicates any of the below orders should take place until achieved (if achieved) or manually canceled by investor.

Limit Order: An order indicating the maximum price to buy or minimum price to sell a security.

Market Order: A buy or sell order placed at the current market price.

Stop Order: An order indicating a specific price to buy or sell a security.

Trailing Stop Order: An order that constantly trails the highest-achieved price by a specific percentage or dollar amount.

INVESTING STRATEGIES

Aggressive Strategy: One that favors single stocks, international stocks, emerging-market securities, and other high-risk investments.

Conservative Strategy: One that favors bonds, mutual funds, ETFs, and other safe investments.

Moderate Strategy: One that favors mutual funds, ETFs, single stocks, and riskier investments.

ABOUT THE AUTHOR

Vishal Reddy has an MBA in finance, but he learned his secrets to investing with his own hard-earned money. Having studied countless books on investing and learned from real-world experience, he brings a wealth of wisdom to readers in One Hour Investor.

CONNECT WITH VISHAL REDDY

Sign up for Vishal's newsletter at
www.vishalreddyauthor.com/free

To find out more information visit his website:
www.vishalreddyauthor.com

Instagram:
vishal_reddy_author

Twitter:
@vreddyauthor

Facebook:
www.facebook.com/vishal.reddy.3910

BOOK DISCOUNTS AND SPECIAL DEALS

Sign up for free to get discounts and special deals
on our bestselling books at

www.TCKpublishing.com/bookdeals

ONE LAST THING...

Thank you for reading! If you found this book useful, I'd be very grateful if you'd post a short review on Amazon. I read every comment personally and am always learning how to make this book even better. Your support really does make a difference.

Search for *One Hour Investor* by Vishal Reddy to leave your review.

Thanks again for your support!

Made in the USA
Coppell, TX
29 January 2022

72642612R00066